The Pastor as Counselor

The Pastor as Counselor

André Godin, S.J.

Translated by
Bernard Phillips

Holt, Rinehart and Winston

New York   Chicago   San Francisco

NIHIL OBSTAT: Rt. Rev. Msgr. James T. Clarke, S.T.L.
Censor Librorum
June 15, 1965
IMPRIMATUR: ✠ Most Reverend Jerome D. Hannan, D.D.
Bishop of the Diocese of Scranton,
Pennsylvania
June 19, 1965

The nihil obstat and imprimatur are official declarations that a book or pamphlet is free of doctrinal or moral error. No implication is contained therein that those who have granted the nihil obstat and imprimatur agree with the contents, opinions, or statements expressed.

Designer: Ernst Reichl
83179-0115
Printed in the United States of America

CONTENTS

The Pastor as Counselor

INTRODUCTION

The Current Position of Pastoral Psychology

UNTIL NOW, the psychology of pastoral counseling has remained a relatively unexplored area of applied psychology.[1]*

In addition, some priests and ministers seem troubled by the idea of applying to pastoral work certain techniques which have become quite normal in the training, scientific research, and everyday work of psychological counselors. Apart from a handful of enthusiasts who make a point of constantly "psychologizing" all their pastoral reports, most people are wary of a "naturalistic" outlook which, they believe, rightly or wrongly, can be detected in some psychological publications that were not aimed at them in the first place.

There is probably some truth in this reaction.

The mere reading of works on psychology, even when it provides intellectual satisfaction, is not the best method of

* Notes will be found at the end of the book, pages 145–182.

improving the quality of psychological contact between a pastor and his counselees. It may even cause the relationship to deteriorate. This is often the case with books devoted to pathology or the study of personality. They are useful to the pastor in broadening the limits of his personal ideas, but books on the study of personality or on elementary psychiatry for the clergy soon accustom him to substituting a system of labels and classifications for the complex task of true mental discernment and moral support. At first, this facility seems tempting, but in the end it spoils contact with the real person by removing him and placing him behind the bars of a conceptual scheme.[2]

A genuine pastoral psychology must be especially severe with those pseudopsychological works from which the reader is supposed to be able to learn the art of making converts, winning vocations, suppressing masturbation, or commanding an audience. Appealing to the urge for power, and promising to yield the secret of influencing people without having to learn how to be open to others, such books are nothing but a caricature of psychological work in general and of pastoral work in particular. Nevertheless, this caricature must still be feared, if only because of the willingness of certain readers to accept it.[3]

The discussions, attitudes, and descriptions in this book are therefore quite unconnected with psychology understood as a study of personality or as a means of influencing people. The author suggests at the outset that the reader, especially if he is a priest, forget the fact that psychology can also become a system of theoretical categories or a set of practical formulas. He will be more helped by works on clinical psychology, understood here as a method (possibly to become a science), that permits us to welcome and accept each individual in the uniqueness of his development and personal history, to sympathize with his struggles, conflicts, and aspirations, to listen to his words and plans, and to discuss them with him. Properly speaking, at the present stage this represents more of an "approach" than a technique.

Yet the reservations and the resistance of the clergy, even to books of clinical psychology, are understandable. These books sometimes have an immense human value, but a specifically religious approach is generally missing.[4] Scientific methods and applied techniques may already have produced excellent results in the scientific study of the laws governing psychological counseling[5] and in the training of counselors for secular tasks such as vocational guidance, counseling, and psychotherapy. But their application to the development and operation of a pastoral psychology is still in an early stage. It will not be accomplished without the co-operation of the clergy. There is a need of small working groups whose members, for the sake of their own development, must agree to examine themselves and to constantly question the psychological quality of their words and actions.

This application of clinical psychology to pastoral work is a difficult and demanding task. It is not just a simple transposition that is required but a radical alteration which will call for a great deal of human prudence and spiritual wisdom before it can be of any use to the clergy as a whole. Since the goals of pastoral work are quite different from those of clinical psychology, some of the techniques used for establishing a satisfactory relationship may have to be modified, or at least used in a fundamentally different perspective.[6]

Patient study of pastoral dialogue, determining its natural and supernatural requirements and its immediate and long-term effects, will one day give birth to a pastoral psychology which would be both a method and a science. Many Christian psychologists are calling for this goal and are willing to co-operate in its accomplishment. It will provide an answer to a real need in the Church today, a need felt by

both the pastor and his counselees: a dialogue capable of
expressing and enriching, on a psychological level, this
supernatural relationship which already, by the grace of
God, unites them in their faith.

These reflections on the current position of pastoral psychology should have already made it quite clear that this
book, far from being a manual of pastoral psychology, is
intended as a simple working instrument or, if you like, as
preliminary spadework. At least it attempts to express correctly the psychological problem of pastoral relations on
three levels: coherent *thought* (Chapter I), correct *attitudes* (Chapter II), and relevant *experiments* (Chapter
III). These essays often reflect the discussions and the
situations analyzed in the work-groups, some of whose
activities will be described in Chapter IV.

This book was written by a priest trained in both psychological and theological disciplines. In it he strives to
remain faithful to the actual conditions and the essential
goals of pastoral counseling: a human dialogue undertaken
and carried out in the name of God. It is intended for all
those who are trying to think, study, or establish, within a
pastoral perspective, a relationship which, at its best, will
be worthy of the participants: two human beings, whose
salvation and spiritual progress depend upon their opening
themselves to the grace of God. Of the two, one tries to
speak in such a way that the other becomes more capable
of perceiving, within himself and without, the echoes of the
divine Word.

                                                    A. GODIN, S.J.

CHAPTER I

Psychology
and Pastoral Care

THE PART played by psychology as a science and as a potential technique in modern pastoral care involves several matters of principle which must be discussed before any attempt at a systematic application can be made.

The reader interested in more concrete analyses or practical applications should turn to later chapters, free to return to examine the theoretical structure upon which they are woven into a coherent doctrine.

1 Arguments For and Against

A discussion
There is a story about two spiritual directors, both invited to the same psychological training session,* who argued for

---

* Further details concerning these training sessions will be found in Chapter IV.

a long time about the advisability of accepting the invitation.

Once the usual superficial arguments had been disposed
of (on the one hand, it would be pleasant to meet the
other members and listen to distinguished speakers; on the
other, it would cost too much money and take up too much
time), the first priest, who was already determined to get
as much as possible out of the coming session, exclaimed,
"Well, even if you won't come, you might at least admit
that you are afraid—afraid of hearing yourself called into
question, afraid of learning the psychological basis for the
routine advice you are so accustomed to giving. As the
psychologists say: You're setting up a resistance."

By no means disconcerted at this point-blank attack, his
friend replied, "Since you seem so taken by psychological
analysis, I'll leave it to you for what it's worth. I won't
even bother to discuss it. But I must say that in your fervor
for taking psychology courses, I believe I detect a disturb-
ing lack of confidence in the spiritual direction you give
as a priest. Between you and me, I wonder if it isn't your
lack of supernatural spirit that is responsible for this desire
to play the psychologist and to offer your counselees so
much more than the simple spiritual development for
which they are asking you."

Unconscious resistance or lack of supernatural spirit

Must the whole question of psychological development
in pastoral training remain blocked by these conflicting
accusations hurled at each other by the partisans and the
opponents of increased psychological awareness in priests?
Conducting a discussion along these lines is as inappro-
priate as attempting to judge a system of philosophy by
arguing from an analysis (even if genuine) of the author's
psyche or from his moral failings.

Here, then, are the usual theoretical arguments offered

in favor of a psychological renewal in pastoral care, together with the objections they provoke.

The phrasing of the three most frequently heard sets of arguments for and against is unfortunately so ambiguous that it would be wise to describe them briefly, before discussing their true significance in a more thorough analysis of the part played by psychology in pastoral work.

Arguments in favor

Man is a whole, say the warmest partisans of a psycho-pastoral renewal. Unlike the psychologists, we have for too long thought only of telling a counselee his moral obligations, clarifying his rational convictions, and countering his objections to the faith. We have grown accustomed to speaking only to his intellect. True, we do occasionally appeal to his emotions but without being sufficiently concerned about their quality. This double intellectual and sentimental appeal seems inadequate, sterile, and obsolete to us today. The time has come for us to deal with the whole man in our pastoral work, to explore the affective and social sources of his human development, and to ease the burden of anxiety, frustration, aggression, and guilt which weighs down his personality, produces his anti-religious prejudices, and acts as a barrier to grace.

The pastoral relationship, they continue, is also a whole; no distinction should be drawn between the psychic man and the moral or religious man. "Soul speaks to soul." What an illusion to believe that this fine phrase is a realistic description of everyday pastoral contacts. Pastoral relations depend essentially upon a dialogue between two whole persons: the pastor, and the person or group seeking advice. Inevitably, the dialogue must take place between personalities that are psychologically and socially determined and thus mutually situated. The psychological defects of a spiritual director (for example, his tendency to dominate or his secret wish to exert a fatherly influence that is not entirely spiritual) have an effect on the purity of his pastoral care (for example, on a counselee's need for passive dependence), just as the unconscious prejudices or unacknowledged motives of a preacher can keep the fullness of the religious message from his congregation.

If our pastoral care, they conclude, is to become properly adapted, we must concentrate on eliminating the pastor's psychic defects and seek an improved understanding of the people in our care. Not only does scientific psychology offer fresh insights to the pastor; it also provides him with increasingly effective techniques for getting to know his flock and for influencing them. Pastoral work which ignored or attempted to do without the discoveries of contemporary psychology would be guilty of betraying its own cause. It is time for the pastor to become once again the *"medicus animae,"* that *physician* of the soul mentioned by the Fathers of the Church.*

Arguments against

The goal of all pastoral work, the opponents of psychology remind us, remains the sanctification of souls. This sanctification is a supernatural gift of God and has no connection whatsoever with the goals of scientific psychology.

Similarly, the theoretical basis of pastoral principles rests on the normative precepts of moral and spiritual theology,

---

* In spite of free will and grace, Saint Gregory of Nazianze considered this cure of souls as partially accessible to science and technology, but according to an infinitely more complicated method which he had no hesitation in comparing to the practice of medicine. He expressed this in terms whose latent determinism is almost enough to frighten us today: "Ars quaedam artium, et scientia scientiarum mihi esse videtur, hominem regere, animal omnium maxime varium et multiplex. Id porro quispiam perspexerit, *si animarum curandarum rationem cum corporum medicina contulerit,* quantoque haec nostra laboriosior quam illa tulerit, expenderit, ac, tum materiae natura, tum artis facultate, tum actus fine, praestantior fuerit" (Saint Grégoire de Nazianze, *Oratio Apologetica,* II, c.16; P.G., XXXV, 426).

not on psychological observation. Also, working methods should be supernatural and only distantly related to adaptation to psychological needs. "When I am weakest, then I am strongest of all," wrote St. Paul (II Cor.12:10).• It is through the infirmities of his apostles, even through their psychological defects, that the voice of God will be most clearly heard, rather than through the shrewd observations of well-adjusted psychologists.

Furthermore, they add, experience has shown that the development of psychology in some countries, especially where psychotherapists are easily available, has not only hampered the work of the Church but has sometimes succeeded in sweeping aside and taking over the functions of priests and ministers.

In short, without wishing to deny the value of the insights which may be gained from psychological research, it should be obvious how delicate and how dangerous it is for a priest to become involved in psychology, and particularly in psychotherapy. There is a serious risk that the pastor will all too quickly undertake tasks which belong to specialists, and thus not only waste a great deal of his own time but also lose the very sense of his religious mission. "Medicus animae," yes: physician of the *soul*, a soul by turns free and enslaved, loving and sinning, before God.•

• The Knox translation has been used for all Old and New Testament references. (Trans.)

• While the hidden motions of the soul inflict wounds far less accessible than those of the body, St. Gregory the Great declares that one need not be ashamed of describing oneself as a specialist—the training, in any case, is far less expensive than that of a physician: "Nulla ars doceri praesumitur, nisi intenta prius meditatione discatur. . . . Quis autem *cogitationum vulnera occultiora esse* nesciat *vulneribus viscerum?* Et tamen, saepe, qui nequaquam spiritualia praecepta cognoverunt, cordis se medicos profiteri non metuunt, dum qui pigmentorum vim nesciunt, videri medici carnis erubescunt" (St. Gregory the Great, *Regula Pastoralis*, Part I, c.i; P.L., LXXVII, 14).

2 Basic Ideas and Principles

Fully effective and systematically organized pastoral care calls for some collaboration with psychology and also with sociology. Sometimes this collaboration will be extrinsic, sometimes intrinsic, but it always takes place on separate, quite distinct, planes.

Pastoral care

In working for the greater glory of Christ, the Church is essentially pastoral. Yet neither apostolic nor priestly work, whether magisterial, ministerial, or administrative, is necessarily pastoral. All these activities can be described as "pastoral," but only when considered in a pastoral perspective. What is this perspective?

The traditional image of the pastor is that of a shepherd leading his flock to green fields and ever better pastures. Such action is very close to *pedagogy*; in fact, the two words have the same etymological significance.

Pedagogy, in the broadest sense of the term, is the art and science for providing the means to ensure that individuals and groups develop as they should. Similarly, apostolic and priestly work can be called *pastoral* insofar as it seeks out and uses the most suitable means for providing individuals and societies with a better idea, a fuller experience, and a richer expression of God's grace.

The pastoral concept, we believe, should always involve a reference to the individuals taken care of,* and especially

---

* According to Father J. de Guibert, this "reference to the individuals" distinguishes Pastoral Theology from Ascetic and Mystical Theology, although the inspiration of both springs from a quest for perfection. He adds: "Pastoral Theology also aims at the personal perfection of the pastor but only insofar as this has a positive effect on his pastoral ministry" (*Theologia Spiritualis*, 4th ed., Ed. Gregoriana, Rome, 1952, p. 7).

to the constant search for improvement in the relations established and developed between men and the sources of salvation. This preoccupation with spiritual growth seems to us to be the distinguishing mark of a specifically pastoral goal. No apostle, especially a priest, is ever satisfied with a mere announcement or repetition of the Christian message, but wants to make sure that it is more fully understood. He is never satisfied with describing or administering the sacraments, but tries to develop attitudes which will ensure their more fruitful reception. Since he is not satisfied with establishing or developing the hierarchical structures of the Catholic community, he makes sure that the institutions are in working order and that they are used by members of the Christian community as additional means of sanctification.*

The pastoral goal is that men "may have life and have it more abundantly" (John 10:10). An action may definitely be considered as pastoral when, using human means, it co-operates with grace to produce an improvement in individuals or in society.

The twofold basis of a pastoral science

Pastoral theology, a systematic and authorized outline of all serious pastoral work, springs from a twofold source.

1) *Normatively,* it is based on dogmatic and moral theology, but it does not share the same goals. In fact, pastoral theology develops principles based on dogma or revelation only insofar as they play a part in the psychologi-

---

* In his Apostolic Letter on the training of the clergy, Pius XI expressed his deep concern that sacred things should be put to a better use as a source of inspiration in pastoral training as such: "Qui ea studia moderatur . . . plurimum tribuet Theologia Pastorali. Nec vero dumtaxat, quam sancta sint divina tractanda praecipiet, sed praeterea quemadmodum sint *maiore semper cum fructu hominibus applicanda*" (*Officiorum Omnium,* August 1, 1922, A.A.S., XIV, 449–458).

cal growth of the individuals or groups whose spiritual progress is involved. From this point of view, pastoral theology is closely linked with the traditional methods by which the Gospel message has found spiritual and dynamic expression throughout history.[1]

2) *Practically,* pastoral theology enlists the aid of all the sciences of human development, especially psychology and sociology, but assigns them a subordinate role.[2] As we shall see, these applied sciences consider the human totality (body and soul) as a totality. When applied to pastoral work (and so far only the most tentative attempts have been made), these sciences do not enjoy absolute autonomy over theology. They have, however, a relative autonomy when they are put to systematic use to discover the appropriate means by which a state favorable to grace can be produced at the different ages and stages of individual and social development.

The twofold movement in a pastoral relationship

Similarly, a genuine pastoral relationship must spring from a twofold movement, requiring strict obedience to a twofold law: the need for *fidelity* and the need for *adaptation.* On the one hand, the pastor must bear constant witness in his personal behavior and in his pastoral methods to a complete fidelity to Christ, whom he represents, and to the Christian values which he preaches in the name of the Church. On the other hand, he must use external means of communication (sermons, conversations, social organizations, personal activity), means which are greatly influenced by the psychology and social position of both the pastor himself and of the people he is speaking to.

It would certainly help pastors to make their testimony more authentic and their teaching more effective if they were aware not only of their moral but also of their psychological shortcomings, and were able to take the necessary steps to correct them—especially those involving relations with the individuals in their charge—thus "setting an example, as best you may, to the flock" (I Peter 5:3). Let us now see how far and on what level scientific psychology can be of help.

Scientific psychology

Misunderstandings easily arise when psychology is under discussion. It is not always sufficiently understood that the object of psychology as an applied science is not the study of the whole man, still less of his higher activities—his intelligence, will, and spiritual sentiments—but the study of the "determined" part of man, that is, those areas conditioned by certain assessable influences, and developed by the action of certain dynamisms operating according to laws as yet unknown. The aim of psychology as an applied science is to isolate these influences and to describe these dynamic processes.

The immediate object of scientific psychology is the psyche, that ensemble of functions, conscious or affecting the consciousness, which are not under the direct control of the will (e.g., innate dispositions, intellectual or affective structures, mental processes, dynamic laws of interpersonal relationships governing the origin and development of groups, etc.). The psyche is thus readily distinguished from the spiritual faculties studied in philosophical psychology by means of reflexive or phenomenological analysis, and also from the bodily changes which doctors and biologists consider (by a process of systematic abstraction) as purely organic or physiological. The true object of contemporary psychology as applied to human beings can be adequately summed up as follows: It is the science of the human composite as a totality, insofar as it functions as a living, psychosomatic, psychosocial whole, intrinsically dependent upon the body and its environment. Modern psychology views this composite in a strictly scientific perspective, attempting to discover the links between antecedents and consequences, to isolate the causal relations and to state the laws of succession for observed phenomena. In this way the idea of *time* appears in its formal object, and this time is that of a living man, not a simple passage from one state to the next, but an irreversible, recapitulative evolution that can be expressed in one word: *maturation.*

Thus, according to these definitions, the conclusions of scientific psychology are always confined to questions of cause and effect (the observed connection between antecedents and consequences); and by its own methodology, all questions of value or ultimate significance are excluded. The psychologist examines psychological conditionings, nothing more. For him, even motivation remains simply "psychological motive" which, scientifically speaking, is not subject to value judgments.[3] As regards the moral order— and, therefore, as regards grace—the data and laws governing mental processes are only determining factors which a philosopher would class with the material causality of human behavior.[4]

The methodology of modern scientific psychology also proves that neither religious psychology nor pastoral psychology is completely autonomous. The religious act takes place essentially on the plane of free will, thus transcending all psychic laws. The same holds true for the pastoral relationship, which, although it is inspired by supernatural motives, actually occurs on the level of interpersonal contact. It is true that scientific psychology studies certain general psychic conditions, or certain mechanisms that operate in all human relationships, and which are connected more or less consciously with the religious life. When a religious science, such as pastoral theology, turns to the data supplied by a psychological science, it adapts this data to its own needs by relating it explicitly to pastoral or religious values, thus transforming something that was merely the science of psychic structures into a religious or pastoral psychology.

It follows, therefore, that psychology enjoys complete methodological autonomy only so long as it remains confined to the study of facts and psychic phenomena. Once the question of its "religious" or "pastoral" significance is raised, it must remain strictly subordinate and dependent.

This principle has many applications. One example is that an interviewing technique of proved psychological effectiveness[5] can be adopted as a pastoral technique only after careful consideration and after the necessary modifications have been made, based on theological doctrine concerning, for example, relations between a spiritual director and his penitent. The technique in question should not be considered for its psychological effectiveness but in relation to the essentially theological nature of pastoral work and the goals of spiritual direction. In the next chapter we will discuss those psychological functions that are essential to pastoral work.

3 The Twofold Relationship
Between Pastoral Work and Psychology

This twofold relationship runs parallel to the theologically determinable connection between grace and psychic dispositions.[6]

1) First of all, an extrinsic relationship in the work of sanctification in its strictest sense. "Essential" sanctity—the presence of sanctifying grace and innate virtues cooperating with the human will—is not intrinsically dependent upon psychic dispositions but upon that spiritual act of surrender by which the human being places himself in the hands of the Holy Spirit, an act inspired by God in union with the Church. Provided that free will has not been entirely suppressed, this act of loving surrender can occur under any psychological conditions, including such neurotic

states as anxiety, scrupulosity, or obsession. Whatever psychic conditions or social influences may prevail, God can, *de jure*, plant the seed of charity in the soul, where it can draw nourishment from the sacraments and develop through acts of supernatural virtue, provided, of course, that a minimum of free will remains.

However, there is no denying the existence of an extrinsic relationship. As in the case of total insanity, there is a sort of threshold beyond which spiritual problems no longer exist—not, at any rate, in our experience. There are also certain psychic dispositions or social influences that are so hard to bear and so compulsive that the chances of a person's persevering along a particular course—for example, in the religious life—are considerably reduced. The same point of view is traditionally expressed in pastoral textbooks: When a priest has to decide whether or not a mental patient may receive the sacraments, there are certain signs which show whether the minimum degree of awareness exists. When someone asks for absolution, there are certain courses to be followed for determining the penitent's essential moral attitude. There are also methods for evaluating external appearances in order to decide, with a reasonable margin of safety, the advisability of a person's being baptized, ordained, or married. In all these instances, psychology plays an indirect, auxiliary, yet extremely important role in helping to clarify the pastor's "prudential" judgments. Improved psychological training can help the priest to detect the symptoms of mild or serious neurosis. In the less serious cases, he can clarify the situation or at least restore the supernatural balance; in the more serious cases, he can refer the person to an appropriate specialist. Even if this was all psychology could do for pastoral work, it would still be an enormous help. But it can certainly do a great deal more.

2) An intrinsic relationship on the level of a full expression of the fruits of grace. The work of grace does not just end with that spiritual event involving the funda-

mental sanctification of a soul or the choice of a way of life. The new life of grace and the engagements entered into under its influence tend to suffuse the entire personality and to radiate out from it.

A spiritual act produces visible results. The relationship with God tends to express itself and to produce human activity (Ephesians 5:3; Galatians 5:16–25). If divine charity is to be implanted more deeply, enjoyed in greater ease and security, and expressed more fully in individuals and in society, it is the human composite as such which must conform as far as possible to those dynamisms which confer grace upon it through the intermediary of free will.

Psychologists study the laws and techniques that govern this psychic development and maturity on the natural plane. We now look to such a maturity in order to ensure the fullness of Christian growth and expression, first, in the pastor, then in every Christian and in the pastoral relationship itself. Psychic qualities in themselves are no guarantee of perfection or Christian virtue, nor do they provide a basis for fruitful pastoral relations. However, they do affect their normal empirical expression and that full maturity necessary for the building up of the Body of Christ.

True, a scrupulous person can achieve sanctity in spite of—and perhaps even because of—his neurosis, but he will bear imperfect witness to others of the reality of divine mercy and of the joyful and confident security which the Christian enjoys.

Similarly, a suspicious, authoritarian priest can offer spiritual advice which will ensure his penitent's faithful submission to God and hence his sanctification. But he will provide very few of the other benefits which should stem from a spiritual director's sense of charity, such as the warm sense of being respected, welcomed, and understood. Thus, pastoral work has no intrinsic need of psychology to ensure the essential sanctification of souls. That is the task of grace. But psychology is necessary if pastoral work is to remain faithful to the outward signs and to the social message of the Word incarnate, drawing all members of the Mystical Body toward that fullness of human and spiritual maturity in their relations to each other and to God.

Even though effective pastoral care is a spiritual mystery and depends upon the workings of grace and the psyche-transcending dialogue between two souls, the pastoral relationship itself must still develop its human qualities in order to serve in this world as an improved instrument and as a guide to the message of the Holy Spirit.

We see, then, the twofold relationship, extrinsic and intrinsic, between fully conscious and systematically ordered pastoral work and psychology. It is also the aim of current attempts at developing certain aspects of psychology that may one day from a true *pastoral psychology*. If these attempts are successful, it will not be the personal sanctity of the pastor that is directly affected, nor that of his counselee, nor yet their relationship, based as it is on faith and prayer. It will be their actual meetings and their dialogue that become improved expressions of divine charity.

None of this will make the pastor's task any easier, but it may bring it closer to reality.

It is not even certain that the pastoral and psychological functions will themselves emerge as complementary. In fact, it is highly probable that they will be diametrically opposed to each other. For the psychologist's approach based on respect, good will, and understanding is often quite different from the fundamentally pedagogical and pastoral approach based on personal conviction, acceptance of a long-term goal, and prudent discretion. The greater his psychological experience, the more the pastor will find himself torn between conflicting spiritual and psychic goals. He will often be forced to limit the psychological aspect of this work, for this is not his field, and he is not directly competent. This will be discussed more fully in Chapter III.

4 Reconsideration of the
Arguments For and Against

If the preceding statements are accepted as valid, they should enable us to deal simultaneously with both sides of the argument outlined at the beginning of this chapter. They will also serve to tone down some of the more outspoken statements and to further an understanding of the true purpose of the discussion. Here they are, in the same order, with the necessary modifications applied.

Arguments in favor

Man is a whole—agreed. But this involves certain "situational" elements which lie beyond the control of free will. Modern psychology teaches us to take certain structures and dynamisms into consideration. The course of moral and religious life must run along these tracks; barring a miracle, it is rarely possible to transform them. Revealing them in pastoral work does not mean working through them; it means placing ourselves in a better position to evaluate their religious significance. As in the past, this will still depend essentially upon moral and supernatural attitudes—an openness to the gifts of the Holy Spirit.

Pastoral relations cannot be established on a purely spiritual level, and any dialogue must always take place between two whole human beings. However, as pastoral theology reminds us, the fundamental aim of this relationship is not a therapeutic interview; the pastor must gradually efface himself in order that the Spirit of Christ may speak more and more distinctly to the soul of the counselee. The formula for this gradual effacement is provided in the Gospel story of St. John the Baptist: "He must become more and more, I must become less and less" (John 3:30). It is not the richness of a well-ordered psychic relationship that is

required but the discretion of authentic spiritual understanding and sometimes a complete withdrawal before the
mystery of the relationship between the soul and God.

Pastoral care involves the correction of psychic defects.
However, this often calls for specialized techniques in
which the pastor is not qualified. All the same, even when
a fundamental change is out of the question, he may, by
appealing to the person's spiritual resources, succeed in
changing the significance of these defects. An example
would be his attitude when faced with a neurotic motivation
toward the religious life, closely linked to the counselee's
infantile psychic apparatus. A typically pastoral form of
psychological aid would attempt to awaken fresh spiritual
motivations which would not be imposed on the old ones
nor suppress them entirely (long-established affective patterns are usually almost inflexible), but would produce a
radical change in their significance.

Arguments against

The goal of pastoral work is the sanctification of souls—
agreed. But this is its ultimate and, so to speak, indirect
end. God alone can sanctify those souls which accept the
freely made offer of His grace. The task of pastoral work,
properly speaking, is to make sure that the necessary means
of sanctification are available so that God's gifts may be
better presented, more surely and more fully assimilated,
and, finally, that they may bear better fruit.

Sanctification in itself depends only extrinsically upon
the conditions studied by scientific psychology. But it does
depend upon them intrinsically in order to improve its
presentation of the means of salvation. It is for this modest
but essential purpose that pastoral work needs certain psychological insights and techniques which it will select and
adapt for its own ends.

The basis of pastoral work is no more purely theological
than its techniques are exclusively supernatural. To repeat:
Pastoral work and the action of divine grace must not be

confused. The pastoral relationship is always "bipolar," just as its basis is twofold and its methods are varied. It is from this twofold source (normative and practical, theological and scientific, moral and psychological) that its particular quality is derived: that of a tool which can be adapted to fit a particular task and altered to match the skill and purpose of the worker using it.

If the voice of God is heard more clearly through the defects of the pastor, this is not because of these defects but probably because of the humility or other moral virtues displayed by the pastor who, in spite of all his efforts, continues to suffer from these defects.

Finally, if a certain historical antagonism exists between the development of certain psychological methods and the priestly influence, doesn't this spring from the fact that these methods were developed in a secular context, far removed from the religious, Christian inspiration which would have revealed their true significance? On the other hand, they have brought a human quality into such secular relationships as interviews with psychologists or psychotherapists, a quality rarely found in relationships with priests. It is therefore understandable that clerical prestige felt threatened or even replaced on the level of human relations by the psychological skill of the counselor or psychotherapist. Cases are often mentioned of people choosing to pay a great deal of money and claiming to be suffering from a nervous disorder, simply to discuss their problems, even their religious ones, in an atmosphere of welcome, understanding, and true insight. This was something they could not find (not, at least, on the level of a dialogue worthy of Christian maturity) with the priests whom they would have preferred to consult, without attributing a magical significance to the priests' role or words. In other words, they made a clear distinction between the priests' role as ministers of the sacraments and their role as pastoral counselors.

Surely it would be most unfortunate to aggravate the

situation by refusing to enrich spiritual dialogue through better study and understanding of the laws that govern it. Would it not be sheer "supernaturalism" to continue to reject training methods which would permit us to offer counselees, even in pastoral work, some of that sympathetic, disinterested attention which laymen demand today? Unless the pastor takes the necessary steps, working systematically toward an improvement in his own attitude in pastoral relations, his own personal sanctity will not provide that prerequisite to all dialogue—an ability to listen skillfully. From a psychological point of view, a refusal to consider these methods would mean holding up the eagerly awaited modern pastoral renewal.

Finally, is there not a graver risk of internal conflicts within the priest himself if psychological preoccupations are added to his moral and theological training? Some have detected a tendency among young Protestant clergymen, especially in the United States, to devote more and more of their time to acquiring an increasingly thorough knowledge of psychological techniques, sometimes even emulating qualified psychotherapists and putting religious values to systematic use in the service of mental health.[7]

First, we must say that no method can be condemned because of abuses of it.

The abuse, if it exists, is most likely to be found in areas where faith in the work of priests and the sacraments properly speaking ("ex opere operato") has practically disappeared from the Christian consciousness. It follows that spiritual salvation (the work of God) and psychic cure (the work of psychological or psychotherapeutic techniques) may become dangerously intermingled. Given these circumstances, it is understandable that some pastors might strive for technical perfection in the very real— though not religious—skills of the psychologist or psychotherapist, if only in an attempt to maintain some hint of that religious significance which the majority of their counselees deny. In this profane, desacramentalized context, such psychological efficiency would cease to be symbolic of that supernatural efficacy—the work of God— which people no longer believe in.

As can be seen, any confusion, as well as any separation, between the sacramental and psychological aspects of pastoral work involves a deadly compromise of the true relation of Christianity to mental health. Both aspects go together: once belief in the efficacy of a priest's sacramental actions has been abandoned, any psychological skills he may have acquired will simply make him into a rival of the psychotherapist and even, in certain cases where his training has been inadequate, into a real "sorcerer's apprentice."

It is essential to revive a strong awareness of the priest's twofold responsibility: his sacerdotal and sacramental responsibility as the bearer of the Word of God and the minister of the supernatural means of salvation; also his pastoral responsibility as mediator of that full maturity of Christian consciences and societies which will not be achieved unless he himself acquires certain techniques (mainly psychological and sociological) and applies them in the Church in the service of priestly charity.

In our opening chapter, we have attempted to show that this mammoth undertaking, a long-term, collective enterprise, even in the modest field of psychological relations, can be brought to a successful conclusion only by a constant awareness of its twofold planes, psychic and religious, in accordance with the fundamental principles of authentic pastoral theology, a pledge of fidelity to the Word incarnate.

CHAPTER II

Psychological Functions of Pastoral Counseling

IN THE previous chapter it was emphasized that the basis, goals, and methods used in pastoral care are rather different from those of a psychological relationship. On the other hand, the existence of a science and technique for an authentic pastoral psychology is quite possible, because pastoral relations themselves are based on universal, observable tendencies, and employ psychic processes that are relatively constant in the pastor, in the people who seek his advice, and in the relationships established between them.

Before examining some actual experiences in pastoral relations, this chapter will be devoted to a discussion of the appropriate psychological attitudes necessary as a basis for a well-established, well-ordered pastoral relationship. Once agreement has been reached on the principal attitudes involved in this relationship, it will be easier to evaluate the quality of a given dialogue, or the relevance of an answer given during an interview, in terms of the desired goals.

Variety of situations

First, we must mention the wide variety of circumstances in which our pastoral aid is often sought. We shall consider the range of these situations again later on.

A priest is summoned to a thirty-year-old spinster who has recently lost her father. She is completely broken up, bitter, and sensitive. She tries unsuccessfully to express herself. When she does, it is to say that she doubts everything: her Christian faith, herself, and other people. The priest knows his theology, but he also responds to this distress. It is now his turn to be tongue-tied by the words of hollow consolation that spring to mind. Quite literally, he does not know "what attitude to take." How can be gain access to the personality of this woman who has asked to see him and is now speaking so openly and honestly? What can he do or say in order to establish a pastoral relationship which will also be psychologically valid?

A young man comes to see the curate. He is thinking of getting married but cannot make up his mind. He has dated several girls without ever establishing a stable relationship. He is obsessed with the idea that certain "guarantees" are needed before one can commit oneself for life. To him, the guarantees always seem insufficient. What does he expect from the curate? Reassurance? A decision made on his behalf? How should such a dialogue be conducted?

A Benedictine is visiting a twenty-five-year-old working man in a hospital. He is an active layman and the father of five children. Instead of the convalescent he was expecting, the priest finds a worried man on the verge of despair. His condition has deteriorated. There is talk of bone tuberculosis. He will probably never recover. "How can God allow such a thing?" What human significance can this situation have? What sort of pastoral aid can be provided?

As a reminder, we mention the classic difficulties of pastoral counseling: masturbation and scruples, scandals within the Church, the sense of suffering, requests for money, for human comfort, and for ready-made solutions.

Obviously, psychology has no prefabricated formulas ready to help the priest deal with each of these situations. Rather, it will suggest that he give extremely careful, personal consideration to his own, immediate, interior reactions to the details of these everyday situations, and compare his own reactions to the attitudes which an authentic pastoral relationship seems to require. These attitudes, intimately bound to the character of the priest as God's "re-presentative," correspond to three main functions which form the basic structure of the priest's pastoral care: welcome, guidance, and mediation.*

1 The Function of Welcome and Acceptance

The first duty of pastoral dialogue should be to provide every counselee with a unique opportunity for being welcomed, accepted, and understood as he is, in the fullness of his intellectual, moral, and affective existence. God's grace can penetrate into human nature at any time and under any circumstances. "And Jesus said to her, 'I will not condemn thee either'" (John 8:11). The good shepherd is not only prepared to give his life for his flock; he knows his sheep and can call each one by name.

This "warm acceptance" of the counselee, a technique

* The following remarks were made and developed in the course of the working groups mentioned in the Introduction. Their scriptural foundation is provided in an occasional text. But their pastoral authenticity springs from the fact that they are a "systematic reflection on the Church's mediations in their work for the greater glory of God." This excellent definition of pastoral theology is borrowed from Father P.-A. Liégé, O.P., "Pour une théologie pastorale catéchétique," in the Revue des Sciences Philosophiques et Théologiques, 39, I (January, 1955), p. 5.

developed in therapeutic school of Carl Rogers[1] and often recommended in social work,[2] involves several aspects.

a) The person must be *welcomed* as he is, as a free agent, in his relationship with us. One should always respect the rate of progress and the limits which he himself sets and gradually alters as the relationship develops. A pastoral relationship generally begins on the counselee's initiative* and will not develop properly unless he is allowed complete freedom. If the pastor attempts directly or indirectly to exert any pressure to induce intimacy, the whole relationship may be endangered.

The hardest and most fundamental aspect of this psychological acceptance is the need to respect the nature of the pastoral relationship as proposed by the counselee and as evolved by him.

b) The person must be *accepted* as he is, with all his difficulties and problems. True pastoral welcome requires complete availability so that we may listen carefully to the attitudes and problems of the other person, seeing them as far as possible from his point of view and empathizing, if not with the proposed solutions (which may be discouraging or wrong), at least with the efforts being made to reach a provisional solution.

Far too often, a hasty reply—even when objectively sound—can give a counselee the sad impression that he has no right to have problems, or, at least, that he has no right to have them for any length of time, or to allow them to mature freely. Far too often, words which should reassure and encourage only irritate or discourage, because they are not pronounced on the basis of a solid relationship of wel-

---

* This is always the case with "spiritual direction." Of course, there are other occasions in pastoral work when the priest visits a person's home on his own initiative. However, it must be recognized that this relationship will not attain full pastoral maturity unless the initiative is eventually accepted and taken over by the parishioner.

come and acceptance. Far too often, excellent advice is not acted upon, simply because it was offered too soon and without any real understanding. This attitude of understanding welcome may even exist, but if the priest never gives it verbal or nonverbal expression, the counselee will never know it or feel it.

From now on, whenever we use the word "acceptance," we do not just mean a state of benevolent receptivity. In pastoral dialogue some form of expression is also required. It is probably on this level of explicit communication that psychological training could produce the best results.

c) The counselee must be *understood*, and he must be made aware of this. He must be understood in his own, unique, inexchangeable individuality, in the uniqueness of his providential destiny. There is a risk here that psychology will serve very little useful purpose in this primary function if it limits itself to deductive systems derived from typology and the study of personality, which are all too often devoted to premature judgments and hasty generalizations. There is much more to be learned in individual clinical psychology, both normal and pathological. Here, one is taught to observe the whole individual, to take part in his struggles, and to understand that behind that section of his life which is being described lies the effect of all the influences that have accumulated within him in the course of his personal development, and of which he is the living result. To understand in this sense is not the same thing as to approve. It is to see the present as the counselee sees it, and to set it against the background of his past so that in it he may perceive the value of his future.

To accept the counselee as he is, to let the pastoral relationship ripen on his own terms and at his own speed, to communicate a sense of welcome and understanding and respect—this is to be our fundamental attitude. Now we will examine it in detail, as expressed in the actual words and phrases used during a counseling session.

PSYCHOLOGICAL ANALYSIS:
THE BEGINNING OF A DIALOGUE

To give a concrete example of the function of welcome, a systematic analysis of an actual pastoral dialogue is required, concentrating on the extent to which each reply transforms or modifies the psychological relationship with the counselee. The value and effect of certain typical responses at the beginning of a pastoral interview can thus be studied and an attempt made to evaluate them, but only from the point of view of the function of welcome and acceptance.

If this function is to work correctly, the counselee must realize that he is being listened to, accepted, and understood:

1) In the relationship that he is establishing with us, of his own free will.

2) In his difficulties and his problems, in his hopes and failures as he has lived and experienced them.

3) In his own providential course, unmarked and uncharted in advance.

With this goal in mind, we should concentrate on the attitudes and the inner world of the counselee; we must see whether the verbal reactions he hears provide a comfortable relationship, whether they give him the greatest possible opportunity of expressing himself as he is, without being limited or in any way discouraged by the untimely reactions of the counselor.

The welcoming function probably plays its most important role at the beginning of the first interview; there is a risk that it may fail, and this will place a heavy burden on the remainder of the dialogue.

Here, then, is the beginning of an interview. Ordinary in itself, it illustrates how any of the pastor's typically possible answers can affect the continuous yet uncertain growth of a relationship.[3]

The beginning of an interview

Jean is thirty years old, the eldest in a family of three children. After her mother's death, she remained at home with her father and her two brothers. Four months ago her father died. First in writing and then over the telephone, Jean has asked for an interview with the pastor "to discuss religion and also my father's death." She comes to the rectory and is shown in to see Father X, who is substituting for the pastor for a few weeks. After the usual polite formalities the conversation begins.

[1] JEAN: *This is why I want to speak to you, Father. Ever since my father's death, life has become extremely difficult. At first, I felt I'd simply taken enough. I was ready to drop everything and go to join him. You swallow something and there you are . . . somewhere else. It's so simple. But* [a rueful smile], *to have done that, I would have had to have known where to find him.*

A long pause tells Father X that Jean will not go on without a reply or some sort of human reaction.

First of all, Father X should be congratulated for not breaking hastily into this long silence but allowing it to run its full course. Learning to listen *in silence* is part of the training of a good pastoral counselor. Scientific observation[4] has shown that young counselors have a tendency to talk too much and too fast. Not only do they collect less data which might help them in their counseling work, they also leave the counselee with the impression that he has not been properly received and listened to. An attentive, silent presence is the most precious gift a priest can first offer a human being who comes to him for help or advice.

Naturally, there must be an intuitive, affective awareness of when the silence has gone on too long and has become awkward, powerless, or ineffective. This judgment must be made in terms of the counselee and not of oneself. In five out of ten cases, especially with beginners, the interruption comes too soon, due to the pastoral counselor's own anxiety: he is burning to speak and to interrupt because of his own sense of insecurity. Just consider our own behavior—we talk more when we are tired, overwrought, or worried, and our remarks are clumsier and less effective.

Now Father X decides to provide an initial verbal reaction to Jean's remarks. At this point, different priests would make different replies. These replies will be called X_1, X_2, X_3, X_4, and X_5.

X_1: *You certainly did very well not to carry out your original idea.*

X_2: *My dear child, there comes a time when we all have to face a similar situation.*

X_3: *Your father has lived his life, but you still have yours to live.*

X_4: *So what did you do?*

X_5: *You must have been terribly upset.*

We will now try to see the probable implication in each of these replies, analyzing each in relation to the welcoming function and trying to grasp its psychological significance in the context of the developing relationship.

X_1: *You certainly did very well not to carry out your original idea.* The essential feature of this first reply reveals a judicial attitude: Jean did very well—but she might have done very badly. The psychological relationship is immediately colored. Jean is talking to someone who judges her replies on the moral plane. She will probably have some difficulty in revealing her thoughts, actions, and plans, knowing that they will have to run the gantlet of this priest's moral judgments. This is not consistent with the idea of true welcome.

It should be noted here that there is no question of excluding a judicial attitude on the part of the priest, for this forms an essential part of the function of pastoral guid-

ance. He is also a representative of an objective order of
values and moral obligations. We only wish to draw attention to this point: Whatever tone is used here,* the word-
ing of the remark implies a judicial attitude. In addition,
we do not consider it the happiest choice for an opening
reply. Moreover, Jean has been totally misunderstood. She
was not talking seriously about suicide. She probably mentioned it, with a sad smile, as an introduction to her real
affective problems following her father's death. X_1 shows
that he has not grasped the human implications of Jean's
remarks. Perhaps the reference to suicide created a block
within himself. Perhaps he was simply too tired or bored,
and automatically fell back on the facile replies of the
complacent moralist.

X_2: *My dear child, there comes a time when we all have
to face a similar situation.*   There is no need to discuss the
dubious display of paternal feeling evident in "my dear
child." After all, tone and expression can carry off many
things and can even justify them. Let us concentrate on the
psychological value of this reply which lies in its quality
as a generalization. X_2 uses the generalization to soothe and
to reassure—so many people, including the pastor himself
perhaps, have been through this before. There is no need
to panic. With the help of God's grace, and a few other
graces as well, everything will be all right in the end, and
so forth.

Obviously, any generalization has certain palliative prop-
erties, and we must know how and when to use them to
soothe growing anxiety. But is *this* the right place for it?
Jean has hardly had time to express herself and here X_2 is
already trying to calm her down. Moreover, any generaliza-

---

* It has been suggested that if this answer was delivered in a bantering,
almost jocular manner, it would lose all judicial value and fill the need for
welcome. Perhaps. But it would hardly match the fundamental seriousness
of the counselee's opening remarks.

tion must involve a colossal coefficient of banality: other people have been through this before—there's no need to panic. In other words (and here I exaggerate deliberately), yours is a perfectly ordinary case. Once again, the counselee's psychological reaction is to feel not really welcome. From the very first, the answers she receives seem to be heading away from the unique qualities of her own situation. But it is precisely the unique nature of her experience that she wishes to discuss. And the need for understanding requires that she be made welcome and invited to say more along the same lines. True, the relationship is not ruined, but something must be done if it is to mature favorably. Jean should be received in some fashion other than with these vague generalizations.

X_3: *Your father has lived his life, but you still have yours to live.* Here we are already giving advice—a sermon perhaps—in any case, exhortation. Examples of this type of reply are legion. For example, *the pain you experience at your father's death can reveal the meaning of your own life.* Or, *all that must be left to the will of God.* Or, *Christ's resurrection helps us to accept our own death and the death of others.* All these answers will be believed. Theoretically, they are all perfectly true, valid, objectively just, edifying, and necessary, considering Jean's condition following her father's death. The question to be asked here is: Is *this* the moment for exhortation and highly theological encouragement? To be more precise, do these answers fill the need for welcome and understanding?

We believe that before a man can make this sort of remark he must (even if he is a priest) have acquired the psychological right to do so. He must have established an adequate relationship on the plane of human communication and understanding. Jean's primary need is not to listen to high-sounding words—that will come later, provided she first has time to express herself.

X_4: *So what did you do?*   Here it is: the cold, apparently neutral question. True, ninety-nine times out of a hundred this sort of question gets the conversation moving. But has any real progress been made in the underlying relationship implicit in all human intercourse worthy of that name? There is a danger that the priest who conducts his counseling using almost nothing but questions (once again, let each of us examine his own conscience) will be incapable of establishing a pastoral dialogue of any richness or depth.

A cold question, we said—really much too cold. All warmth of interest and welcome is missing, yet this is so essential at the beginning of a pastoral dialogue.

The question is, we repeat, apparently neutral. This may seem like hairsplitting, but we must point out that the question is not completely neutral, since it suggests continuing the conversation along active lines ("So what did you *do?*") rather than emotional or spiritual ones. Is X_4 an activist, then? Or is he himself wary of giving expression to affective difficulties? In this case, he would do well to postpone any further regular consultations with women, for he is incapable of providing the human and supernatural security they need.

There are other expressions which have the same interrogative effect: *Perhaps you would like to tell me a little more about how you felt, then?* Quite apart from the fact that this rather earnest invitation steers the conversation abruptly into the sentimental and emotional fields ("how you *felt*"), it will have little positive impact. After all, the purpose of Jean's visit was to tell the priest "a little more"; his phrase will not improve the quality of the initial contact being formed between them.

X_5: *You must have been terribly upset.*   Simple words of welcome, calmly spoken, but they have an astonishing effect. In order to appreciate their real value, Jean's opening remarks should be read again. It will be seen that they have not only been heard but accepted, and the meaning behind the words has been understood. Quite calmly and without exaggeration, the priest has grasped, identified, and exactly reflected the feelings that Jean was attempting to express with her clumsy allusion to suicide. This reflection is the fundamental technique of all verbally expressed understanding.

Anyone who occasionally attempts to reflect the words, ideas, explicit feelings, and especially the underlying emotion in the counselee's words will soon see how difficult, yet at the same time how rewarding, it is.

Few counselors manage to develop and maintain the permanent attentive quality required to achieve accurate reflection, affective openness, and a mental availability to other people. It is a question of listening to what is being said and, at the same time, at every instant of the dialogue, intuitively grasping the significance and the affective tone of the words that have just been spoken.

We believe that even experienced counselors fall into two categories: those whose mental affective attitude is almost incurable, who are incapable of seeing anything but the material content of someone else's difficulties and problems; and those whose affective attitude is excellent, but who are incapable of expressing in words the charity, the good will, and the empathy that lies within them, uniting them to the counselee. The latter would have a great deal to gain from a systematic and, if possible, supervised application of reflective techniques. Despite their shyness, they will find in themselves unsuspected capacities for welcome and sympathy. They will see their intimidated counselees beginning to approach them with a previously unheard of confidence and spontaneity. Not only will this improve the psychological quality of their welcome, but the efficacity of their other pastoral functions (moral example and spiritual mediation) will also be immeasurably increased.

Obviously there is nothing absolute about X_5's words.

A hundred other different expressions of reflection and warmth could be used in their place. *You still haven't recovered completely from this terrible shock* has almost the same value, but it lightly tinged with impatience. *You've been through a time of real despair* is also an exact reflection, although here the situation is made to seem worse, and the use of the past tense is perhaps a little premature. *To lose your father in your situation must be a terrible ordeal.* In spite of the obvious attempt to express welcome and understanding, there is a hint of intellectual generalization which will not escape the reader of the preceding analyses. There are many other possible reflections of uneven quality, everything being a question of tone, degree, and authenticity in the actual relationship.

A dialogue in progress

The counselee, encouraged by X_5, is going to go on with the dialogue. In any case, she will feel the effect of the counselor's first reply.

[2] JEAN: *I feel much better now. But I don't know what to believe or think. Until my father's death, everything seemed perfectly clear. I believe in God, you know, but before this I don't think the strength of my faith had ever been put to a real test.*

Her first words suggest that X_5's reflection was accurate— yes, Jean had been "terribly upset." But there are signs here that she is slightly on the defensive, afraid that she has been too well understood and that she gave the impression of too deep a distress. But instead of seeking reassurance from the priest as suggested by X_1 and X_2, it is she who reassures him: "I feel much better now." Also, she herself moves on to the religious aspect of the interview. Accepted in her psychological distress, she does not rest there, but approaches the problem of her belief in God.

She approaches it timidly, as if fearing a reprimand from the priest: "I believe in God, you know." Once again, an answer of complete acceptance is required. Father X provides it.

Father X: *You feel as if you're in a state of doubt.* A perfect reply from the point of view of wholehearted welcome, which is what concerns us here. The priest fully accepts something that she could express only with hesitance. The conversation makes immediate progress, and Jean prepares to describe her psychological and spiritual condition in greater detail.

[3] JEAN: *Yes, that's it. I have doubts. About life, about myself, about everything. I don't think I can ever live and act again as I used to. I don't have enough confidence to face life. I don't think I will ever believe again in the way I did before.* (Silence.) *It's terrible to realize that your faith is no use to you, that it doesn't increase your courage.* (Silence.) *I can't talk about all this at home; it's not easy to talk about these things with the rest of my family.* (A long silence.)

Father X: *So you wanted to talk to someone else about it all.*

[4] JEAN: *Exactly. The idea of speaking to you came to me the other day during that sermon you preached about "naked faith," about people who go on believing after all their reason for believing, all their internal security and all their joy in the faith have vanished. I'll admit that it's possible for priests. But do you think that might be what has happened to me? That I must go through this . . . almost mystical experience?"*

We will now halt our account of this dialogue. The reader can work out for himself* the reply he would or

* Will the priest decide to answer Jean's question? How, at this juncture, can he still comply with that welcoming attitude which tries to follow rather than to lead the counselee while at the same time helping him to clarify his problem? The reader can compare any reply he himself may have attempted with one proposed by a correspondent in note 5.

could make to Jean at this stage. He should try to evaluate
his answer, not only according to the preceding analyses
and the following comments but in relation to his own
psychology and the replies which come most naturally and
most frequently to his lips. Without this process of self-
interrogation, no progress is possible. Each one of us has
his own individual keyboard, but generally we only use a
few of the keys and they are always the same ones: exhorta-
tions, reassuring speeches, commands, theological or moral
formulas, and even (not without risk) human affection or
sympathy, and so forth. All progress in pastoral dialogue
consists of extending the range of our own keyboard, and
using certain keys in terms of the counselee's needs and not
of the counselor's own subjective frame of mind.

Commentary on this dialogue
    The most striking thing about this dialogue is the rapid-
ity with which the central, religious theme is approached.
Within four exchanges the heart of the matter has been
reached, and the dialogue immediately becomes a pastoral
one. No time is wasted on gossip, social chatter, or psychological commiseration. Quite calmly and directly, they go
straight to the topic which deserves the attention and needs
the care of the priest as a priest. This will often be the
result of the reflection technique and the welcoming attitude we suggested as essential at the beginning of any
pastoral relationship.
    Let us now reread these three perfectly appropriate
replies to the counselee's remarks:

To Jean [1]: *You must have been terribly upset.*
To Jean [2]: *You feel as if you're in a state of doubt.*
To Jean [3]: *So you wanted to talk to someone else
about it all.*

The last reply, affectively somewhat noncommittal, com-
pletes the work of the first two: a human relationship has

been securely established beneath the signs of acceptance and understanding. Because they revolved exclusively around the counselee's present situation and his actual needs, these three replies have created an atmosphere of confidence within the first few minutes.

Grammatically even, these three replies demonstrate the correct technique or attitude: they all begin with "you," showing that the pastor's line of reference begins with the counselee. Now we do not wish to be misunderstood; we have no intention of outlawing from the pastoral dialogue any reply beginning with "I." This type of mechanistic formula has never helped anyone. All the same, we would suggest a brief examination of (psychological) conscience. Research has shown that it is those who are most concerned with themselves and the most egocentric in their dialogue who most frequently use phrases referring to themselves.* In a period when literary critics often use semantics and even verbal statistics to uncover and reveal the interior world of the great authors, it is perhaps permissible to suggest that pastoral counselors improve themselves by a modest use of this modern form of examination of conscience.

The pastoral interview with Jean progressed rapidly toward its religious goal because of a correct interior attitude on the part of the pastor and his correct use of welcoming techniques. In order to appreciate this more fully, it should be compared with other possible replies to Jean [2]. We will now examine four of the most common replies, and attempt once again to analyze the implications of each one from the point of view of the functions of welcome and understanding.

For instance, *I hope you won't remain in this state of*

---

* In fact, the research mentioned concerns verbal exchanges between neurotics in therapy. As their affective condition improves, so their egocentric preoccupations are reduced, together with the number of first-person statements.[6] Any application of this to statements made by the pastoral counselor remains quite empirical, but the statistical confirmation is beyond question.

doubt for too long would have been a real psychological
catastrophe. Jean would have lost her right to have problems and to discuss them. The pastor with his "I hope"
thrusts himself into the foreground; he moralizes and gen-
eralizes simultaneously. He could hardly have done better
if he wanted to get rid of Jean for good within ten minutes.

*My child, faith is a gift of God and we must never doubt
God* combines a demilecture in theology with a demi-
sermon. But as far as this interview and Jean's religious
future are concerned, its value seems pretty low. Although
this reply is objectively true, it does not show one jot
of understanding. Undoubtedly, this is why the pastor
attempts to correct it with his rather pat reference to spiritual paternity ("my child").

*Do you mean to say that when your father was alive your
faith was not a genuine faith?* Or: *What do you mean
exactly by the strength of your faith?* Hidden behind these
extremely theoretical and downright embarrassing questions there is certainly an element of understanding and
genuine welcome. But, if I may say so, it is a welcome in
reverse. The pastor as a good theologian has certainly
grasped the problem but in a thoroughly intellectual manner, and now the whole burden of the problem is back on
Jean's shoulders. The least to be said is that these replies
are extremely foolhardy; if Jean has the slightest problem
in the future, then the pastor will find himself in a real
impasse. Who is to decide whether or not Jean's faith was
genuine when her father was alive? And why bring up this
knotty little psychotheological problem in front of the
counselee?

Can you tell me how your doubts began? This would not
be a bad reply; at least it follows the line of direct questioning. It shows understanding and interest, even if the perspective is psychological and intellectual, more appropriate
to a psychotherapeutic examination (anamnesis) than to
pastoral welcome. Moreover, it is always better to let the

counselee explain himself after a sound relationship based
on real understanding has been established, rather than to
press him for an explanation.

It is easy enough to imagine some replies to Jean [3]
which are well wide of the mark. The more or less aggressive allusion to the other members of the family ("I can't
talk about all this at home") is often picked up and emphasized by many spiritual counselors. Father X should be
congratulated on his sober, almost noncommittal, reply:
So you wanted to talk to someone else about it all, hinting
at future mediative pressures. After all, Father X will not
be a true pastor unless he prevails upon Jean to direct her
steps toward the only Person who can be her ultimate
interior witness. *Vivit in me Christus*.

Summary

At the end of this somewhat detailed analysis of the
beginning of a pastoral counseling session, the reader may
wish to take his bearings.

He has met and evaluated the main obstacles to understanding and welcome: a judicial attitude, abstract exhortation or moralization, and intellectual or even psychological
cross-examination.

He has also been able to judge the amazing effectiveness
of reflection, that intuitive reply which echoes back to the
counselee everything he has said and more besides, the
underlying affective tonalities which obscure his vision of
the problem and sometimes paralyze all contact with the
counselor.

Experience has proved that this type of analysis can be
immensely helpful to pastoral counselors who are genuinely
anxious to improve themselves, provided always that they
do not start hunting for ready-made formulas, procedures,
and techniques. Even a valuable method such as the reflec-
tive-reply is useless (and unusable) unless it expresses an
ability to see the other person as he sees himself (empathy),

and an attitude toward him of complete and unconditional receptivity. As with all techniques of human relations, it is inadequate and even dangerous unless it is based on that welcoming attitude of mind required by the primary psychological function of pastoral dialogue.

Moreover, when seen from the perspective of actual religious symbolism, this attitude of acceptance is eminently pastoral. It invites every man to emerge from his isolation, to recognize and accept himself in the presence of another human being who, even if he cannot be that "Judge by whom all men would be judged,"[7] does at least try to display some of his qualities, imperfect as they may be. Besides, this attitude is becoming increasingly rare in our contemporary mass culture. If this warm understanding is gradually disappearing from our increasingly mechanized and socialized world, if it has been hopelessly compromised by the superficiality of all those smiling, administrative "welcomes" by which people try to combat the solitude of men lost in the immense crowds, then there is all the more reason to seek the fraternal understanding and welcome which one man is here trying to provide for those who have recourse to him in the name of God and divine charity.

2   The Directive Function

Like any other man, the priest bears witness to certain values in his pastoral relations. Even if he cannot claim to set an adequate personal example in his own life, his very clothing shows that he is there to bring closer and make more accessible to Christians the religious truths and moral obligations to which they subscribe and to which they are bound. "Go and do not sin again," said Christ after refusing to condemn the woman taken in adultery.

This function of spiritual direction is also essential to the pastoral relationship and is both instructive and elevating on the moral and religious plane. It is, moreover, the one which is most spontaneously exercised by the priest and most requested by his counselees. It forms part of his role and is echoed in his title: spiritual "director." The main problem is to articulate this function correctly with the other two: wholehearted welcome and mediation.

The directive function should not ride roughshod over the other two and, as a general rule, it will be most effectively realized if the following rules are observed:

a) A pastoral interview is not usually based on recourse to a superior with the power to command* or to legislate the behavior of others on the grounds of religious obedience.[8] Moreover, in many cases the actions or states of mind in question are not sinful, nor do they involve moral obligations. Dialogue calls for a prudent choice following careful investigation of the various courses of action that are available.

In this investigation, the pastor must take care to elucidate and clarify, examining with the counselee the various acceptable solutions, providing him with a greater sense of security, and making him more capable of making his own decisions, using his own free will, the legitimate source of all his actions. In order to become a true counselor in the religious sense of the word, it would be wise to avoid the giving of actual advice, however excellent the advice itself may be.

b) Even where moral values indicate a certain course of action, pastoral advice should avoid the use of moral constraint or psychological pressure. Obviously in some ex-

---

* Once again, it is "spiritual direction," or "pastoral counseling," that is being referred to. Of course, pastoral duties can include authoritative measures: warnings, remonstrances, and even judgments. But these three instances are quite rare in contemporary society. As for the vow of obedience and the relations it implies between superiors and subordinates, this involves a very different relational psychology and dialectic, the detailed discussion of which lies beyond the scope of this book.

tremely rare cases (that is, when someone starts talking about suicide, or contemplates a decision involving disastrous social consequences), the pastor should use all his powers of persuasion, throwing the whole weight of his prestige into the balance and not hesitating to protect the future by a real, if temporary, coercion. But he should not yield to the temptation to make this the normal treatment of all well-balanced adults who turn to him. He should remember that the directive function requires him to help his counselees comply with moral norms, not only outwardly but with a free acceptance of them. This would make possible an interior development inspired by the most mature and the most spiritual motivations of which they are capable.

From the point of view of the directive function with which we are now dealing, it is just as important, and sometimes even more important, to improve the quality of the counselee's motivations and to develop a mature foundation for belief and action than to immediately attempt to ensure satisfactory behavior. A moral law always applies; however, its obligatory nature remains dormant if a person's conscience is unaware of it. Once the theoretical basis of an obligation or prohibtion has been established, the directive function involves a patient investigation of the dispositions necessary to ensure the best possible awareness of it.

c) Finally, care must be taken in prolonged pastoral guidance not to induce in the counselee a sense of dependence or passivity in the making of decisions which would result in a total alienation of his moral consciousness and might well stunt his religious growth. This is a particularly pronounced risk in the case of pastors with dominating, authoritative, or pseudopaternal inclinations. As if by chance, they will see a crowd of anxious faces circling around them, the scrupulous and the weak, who ask nothing better than a chance to shed before God the burden of normal responsibility which is the lot of every psychologically mature adult. The psychic discord between the pastor and his counselee may be too intense, and prevent the third function of mediation from coming into play, thus depriving the directive relationship of its essentially religious character.

The third aspect of the directive function in its pastoral application is to develop the psychological autonomy of the counselee in such a way that he constantly submits himself more and more to God's will and adopts divine charity as his center of reference.

The counselee must be encouraged to make his own decisions; he must be permitted to express himself in an atmosphere of security and to develop his personal motivations at his own pace. A relationship should be established that is quite divorced from any sense of psychological superiority or weight of authority, in order to increase autonomy and develop a sense of spiritual dependency, not on the counselor but on Christian realities and values. These are the goals of the second fundamental function of pastoral dialogue.[9]

We will now examine an application of the directive function, satisfactory from both psychological and pastoral points of view, by analyzing extracts chosen from the beginning, the middle, and the end of a typical interview.

PSYCHOLOGICAL ANALYSIS: A REQUEST FOR ADVICE

These sections of the dialogue were chosen because 1) the question asked is genuinely complex; 2) no obligatory standards seem immediately applicable; 3) a strong personal opinion is aroused in the counselor in favor of a solution that is probably better in itself, but which he will, as a good counselor, avoid imposing by virtue of his superior position or by using direct influence. However, this opinion need not necessarily remain unspoken; it can even be effectively expressed, provided the counselee does not have an unreasonable or excessively high opinion of the counselor's advice. In the course of this dialogue, the efforts made by the counselor to respect the counselee's motivations and to let them develop of their own accord will seem particularly praiseworthy toward the end of the interview when the counselee, probably without being fully aware of what he is doing, renews his attempts to extract a clearly defined opinion from the counselor.

It will be obvious that with a request for advice, the dialogue follows a clarifying course which is by no means inconsistent with the function of welcome as discussed in the previous section. The technique employed is suited to the intellectual formulation of the objective situation and subjective motivation.

A request for advice: the beginning of the interview

Mr. Wilson is thirty-six years old, an engineer and the father of three children. He has come to ask the advice of his old high-school teacher, Father Y. After the usual polite remarks, he broaches the reason for his visit.

[1] WILSON: *I don't know whether you've met my son Henry. He's twelve years old, and in a few months he'll be starting high school. Believe it or not, I've been having trouble with our pastor on his account. I want to send him to the new public school, which is only a five-minute walk from our house. But the pastor thinks that a good Catholic should send his children to a Catholic high school. This would involve a thirty-five-minute train ride, not counting the ten-minute walk from our house to the station. Personally, I don't feel conscience-bound to do this. What do you think?*

We will now examine the various replies made by different counselors to this explicit question.

Y_1: *I don't expect your pastor wanted to make this into a case of conscience for you.*

Y_2: *I can't say yet. Tell me more about this new high school. Do you know any of the teachers? Or the principal?*

Y_3: *I see. This is certainly a classic problem in our country. I have already had several old pupils in the same position. Their experiences should help us solve your problem.*

Y_4: *My opinion is unimportant. What do you and your wife think? That's what counts.*

Y_5: *You've got a decision to make, and your opinion doesn't match your pastor's. So you've come to your old teacher for moral support.*

Let us now examine the latent implication or concealed techniques in each of these replies:

Y_1: *I don't expect your pastor wanted to make this into a case of conscience for you.*   A categorical judgment. The counselor thinks clearly and accurately, and he says what he thinks. But there may be insufficient basis for his categorical remarks. How does he know what the pastor's intentions were? Moreover—and this is probably more important—his answer implies that he will settle the question himself. The counselee need only present the remaining factors in the problem and the answers will soon appear. All he then has to do is to act on them, if he wants to (naturally).

Y_2: *I can't say yet. Tell me more about this new high school. Do you know any of the teachers? Or the principal?*   An exploratory reply. This counselor is more prudent. He recognizes that the situation is complex, and requests additional information. But his answer implies that it is he who will choose the necessary data for the solution of the

problem. In any case, the counselee will realize that it is
the counselor who is undertaking the examination of the
problem. He tends, therefore, to feel like a witness under
cross-examination, and if the dialogue continues for any
length of time along these lines, he will be firmly established in the passive role.

Y_3: *I see. This is certainly a classic problem in our country. I have already had several old pupils in the same position. Their experiences should help us solve your problem.*
A reassuring generalization, the counselor boasts of his wide
experience. His generalization reduces the counselee's problem to the commonplace, and hints at a solution that will
exclude from the case any element of originality, its personal character, and perhaps even its real religious content.
In spite of the use of the plural ("should help *us* solve this
problem"), there is a definite impression that it is the
counselor alone who will provide a solution.

Y_4: *My opinion is unimportant. What do you and your
wife think? That's what counts.*   A theoretical explanation, coupled with the abrupt introduction of a theme not
mentioned by the counselee ("your wife"). And all the
work, one feels, is still going to be done by the counselor
(as with Y_1 and Y_2). Yet the counselor's idea is a valid
one. Only it would be preferable to establish the sort of
relationship which would lead the counselee into actually
realizing that "it is what I think that counts," and not one
where he hears it said and also sees the question of his
wife's opinion anticipated.

Y_5: *You've got a decision to make and your opinion
doesn't match your pastor's. So you come to your old
teacher for moral support.*   Here we have a threefold reflection, summary, and clarification of the initial situation as
revealed in the counselee's opening remarks. Note that most
of this reply concerns Mr. Wilson's motivation in seeking
advice, and constitutes a warm acceptance of the entire
problem as it has been posed.

[2] WILSON: *But the thing that complicates the problem in my case is that my wife allows the pastor to intimidate her. You know, she has always been a bit of a worrywort. For her, the children's religious future is a terrible hill to climb. So if there's the slightest hitch in the high school, all the blame will fall on me!*

Y_1: *Naturally, you must make this decision together.* Once again, a categorical judgment. Counselor Y_1 is thinking clearly again and saying what he thinks. In fact, one aspect of the problem has already been disposed of: the relationship with the Wilsons' pastor, one aspect of the exclusively religious dimension of the problem. The counselor is also ignoring the entire affective content of Wilson's second remark: his wife's temperament and his own fear of her future accusations.

Y_2: *Naturally, you must explain your wife's position in greater detail. Has she adopted the pastor's point of view completely?* Explorative with the latent implication: keep on giving me details, and sooner or later an answer will emerge.

Y_3: *Naturally, this is the type of decision which women are often afraid to make, preferring to suspend their judgment until a later date. But no real blame can be laid on someone who takes precautions and acts for the best.* A generalization. The counselor is trying to reassure the counselee by taking refuge behind generalities and abstract principles. He also displays an unfortunate amount of aggression against women: a clumsy attempt at relieving the husband of his worries without reconciling him with his wife.

Y_4: *So the real reason for your perplexity is probably your wife's opinion.* A theoretical explanation. The counselor sums everything up as if he had already reached the heart of the problem. In this sense, his answer is an extremely poor interpretation of a psychological problem that is probably far more subtle.

Y$_5$: *Naturally,*[*] *in the decision to be taken now, you also sense a threat of repercussions in future relations with your wife.* Acceptance and elucidation, shedding fresh light on a new aspect of the counselee's indecision: fear for the future of the conjugal relationship itself.

Here, then, are the five "types" of reply: *evaluation or judgment; exploration; generalization; theoretical explanation or interpretation; elucidation or clarification.* These all come up again at a later stage in the same dialogue. This time we will attempt to see how each one through a psychological process, produces a long-term reaction in the counselee which will be described in the commentary.

A request for advice: the middle of the interview

[21] WILSON: *Of course I realize that my decision should not be made in reaction to my wife's opinion, heavily influenced as this is by the pastor, but that I should consider my son's religious future. This is where I need your advice. Since there is a chaplain at the high school, and religious courses are taught, don't you think he would receive just as good a religious education there as at the Catholic school?*

After each of the different counselor's replies, we have inserted a specimen remark illustrating the line that the counselee will probably take in his next answer.

Y$_1$: *Certainly not! A religious education is a question of atmosphere, not courses in religion. So-called secular subjects must be taught in a religious perspective. Do you be-*

* Four of these five replies begin with the word "naturally," but in each case the word has quite a different meaning. If each phrase is examined in its context, the differences will immediately become obvious. When Y$_1$ uses the word "naturally," he means "it is essential"; Y$_2$ means "please"; Y$_3$ means "I agree with you"; and Y$_5$ means "I understand you." If, as the old saying goes, it is the tune which makes the song, it is the context of the other words which gives this adverb its meaning. It must be said that these shades of meaning are readily observable in actual dialogue, and play their part in structuring relationships between speakers.

lieve that history or literature can be taught in a religiously "neutral" spirit? Believe me—from a religious point of view it would be better for Henry to go to the Catholic school.

WILSON [22] replies: *Yes, perhaps, for the religious atmosphere at the Catholic school. But then there's the question of commuting by train. There's been quite a lot of trouble on those trains—almost riots, and boys no older than Henry have been involved. They probably think they have to imitate some of the young toughs. My sister even talks about a real moral danger . . .*

Y_1 here reaps where he has sown. By constantly stating his own opinion, he has provoked a contrary one. The chances are good that the interview will continue along the following lines: The more arguments the counselor advances in favor of the Catholic school, the more arguments the counselee will find in favor of the local high school. And what is more, he will be increasingly convinced by the reasons he himself brings up *against* the counselor's opinion.

This is often the result of categorical judgments—the relationship is structured on a frame of affirmation and objection. Each speaker becomes firmly entrenched in positions having but the remotest connection with religious motivations.

Y_2: *Who is the chaplain at the high school? Perhaps I could see him and discuss Henry's case?*

WILSON [22] replies to Y_2: *I would be so grateful if you would. In fact, it seems to me that the chaplain would be the best qualified to give an opinion about Henry's religious future, assuming, of course, that he enters the high school.*

Y_2 also reaps where he has sown. Constantly preoccupied with the external details of Mr. Wilson's motivation and his indecision, he substitutes himself for Wilson in the examination of the facts, finally preventing him from making his own decision, which must henceforth depend on a third party, who is probably less likely to understand Henry's family position.

The usual result of a dialogue proceeding by a minute investigation of external facts is the gradual surrender of the decision to persons or events which do not belong in the counselor-counselee relationship. The counselee is referred back to another set of circumstances before any true maturation has taken place in the present dialogue. On the contrary, he is urged to abandon all responsibility for his decision and surrender it to an outside interest. With this alienation, or transfer of responsibility, the whole purpose of the directive function of the interview is lost.

Y_3: *It is generally agreed that the religious awakening is better handled in Catholic institutions. Only the other day I was reading about some research carried out among seniors in the two systems which shows that . . .*

WILSON [22] replies: *But don't forget that if anything is missing from the high school's religion courses, Henry will be able to make up for it at home. The priest I mentioned visits us once a month, and . . .*

Y_3 is faced with the usual result of a generalization. The counselee is not satisfied with this evasion of his individual problem. He is vaguely aware of this dissatisfaction and expresses it (quite rightly) by saying that his own case is quite different and special.

To generalize is, therefore, to by-pass the opportunities presented for motivational development. It will also weaken the interpersonal relationship by by-passing the persons involved. And, finally, it will considerably reduce the power of the dialogue to strengthen the faith of the counselee, who does not feel free, let alone encouraged, to express himself as he really is.

Y_4: *Do you expect me to side with the high school against your pastor?*

WILSON [22] replies: *No, of course not. I understand perfectly. You must excuse me. It's true. I should have realized that you are a teacher in a Catholic school, too.*

Y_4's credit as a psychological counselor is now running extremely low (temporarily, at any rate). By constantly harping on a theoretical interpretation (in this case of the relationship itself), he no longer sees things from the counselee's point of view, and has abandoned all attempt at improving his true motivations. He has his own point of view, and is astonished because the counselee failed to realize this earlier. He is thus a two-time loser as a psychological counselor: first because he abandons the search for a solution with the counselee, and secondly because he compromises the relationship and loses the confidence of a man who had, in fact, believed that he could come to him with an opinion differing from that held by his pastor.

Y_5: *Looking at things solely from the point of view of Henry's religious development, you are asking me to reconsider with you the advantages and disadvantages of the local high school.*

WILSON [22]: *Yes. Look here, they often say that the courses in religion are not the most important part of a Christian education. The ambiance, the atmosphere, the spirit, in which the teachers approach their subjects—these all count. In fact, I wonder whether this isn't the more fundamental consideration, more important even than the essentially "moral" aspect of the railroad journey which worries my wife so much, as well as my sister, who is Henry's godmother.*

Y_5: *Your concern for ensuring the best possible education for your son as a Christian should certainly outweigh other less favorable considerations, from the moral point of view. All the same, if he went to the local school, it might protect him from some undesirable influences.*

Y_5 here reaps the welcome reward of his own patient technique: reflection and clarification. Having constantly followed the counselee's train of thought, having understood, supported, and clarified him, he now hears the counselee himself making the same remarks as the hasty counselor Y_1, who then saw them countered with fresh objections.

This careful "progress," in which the counselee himself gives expression to the succeeding and increasingly elaborate phases of a prudent decision, is one of the most precious fruits of the directive function. This avoids the impasse of a discussion where each party becomes more and more bogged down in his own position, and clears the way for an explanation of different opinions.

Notice also that in Y_5's last statement he manages to maintain a careful balance when he "sums up" between the two alternatives. Y_5 cannot therefore be accused of making a choice in Mr. Wilson's presence, for in so doing he would risk making it in his place.

The counselor will have to undergo one final assault on this subject at the end of the interview. This time we will quote only the answers most likely to produce the best religious motivation in the position that is finally adopted.

A request for advice: the end of the interview

[31] WILSON: *I really shouldn't waste any more of your time and patience. At least it's possible to talk to you. My wife will be pleased to hear everything you've told me. But—to sum things up—what should I do about Henry?*

[31] Y: *To sum up: We have been discussing what you and Mrs. Wilson should do to ensure Henry's Christian education.*

[32] WILSON: *If I understand you correctly, you leave me free to do as I see fit.*

[32] Y: *Of course, since you are trying to provide Henry with the best Christian education.*

[33] WILSON: *Yes, and I believe Henry's Christian education will be better taken care of at home with the help of the local high school chaplain, whom we will invite over,*

than by letting Henry roam the streets and trains for two hours a day for six years.

[33] Y: So in your case, you do not believe that you are conscience-bound to follow the advice of your pastor?*

[34] WILSON: One is always afraid to make this sort of decision. I can understand my wife when she tells me it is pride that makes me want to play such an important part in my son's education.

[34] Y: You are wondering whether it is simply so that God might keep all his influence over your son that you choose the high school which has just been built only a stone's throw from your house.

[35] WILSON: Yes. Still, you wouldn't say I was wrong if I sent my boy to the public school?

[35] Y: After everything we've said you are certainly going to be fully aware of all the factors involved before you make your decision.

[36] WILSON: After talking to you I can see that there are many more factors involved than I would have thought. It really is very difficult.

[36] Y: Yes. It must seem very difficult to you. In Henry's case, there are so many factors to be considered.

[37] WILSON: Yes, but how am I going to make the best choice?

[37] Y: When we come down to it, there are two courses of action open to you—to provide Henry with the atmosphere of a Catholic school, but this requires your son's commuting which worries you and your wife. Or you, your family, and the chaplain must labor to strengthen his religious culture. You must think hard about this twofold perspective. Try to see things from the point of view of God and his plan for us. That is how your best decision should be made.

---

* This remark is made as a good-natured observation and does not involve any judgment, let alone any reproach. It is certainly possible to say it in this way.

[38] WILSON: *We will think it over. I'll let you know what we decide. Thank you very much. You have really helped me to see things much more clearly. I would never have imagined that my desire to see Henry go to the local high school could have concealed a tendency to control him myself. Still, whatever happens, I hope he turns out to be a fine Christian.*

[38] Y: *From now on, that is going to depend more and more upon him. All we can do is to provide for our children as best we can. After that . . .*

[39] WILSON (at the door): *Yes. After that it's up to God. Goodbye, Father. I'll write and tell you what my wife and I decide.*

Every attempt made by Mr. Wilson to make the counselor adopt a definite position has met with the same indefatigable attitude: he has reflected the problem, clarified it, summed things up, repeated the alternatives, and thus raised the level of the debate, but always at the counselee's own speed and rhythm. One point which should be emphasized is the excellent summary of the possible alternatives at Y [37] ("When we come down to it, there are two courses of action," etc.). Even if the counselor does add something here, it is nothing but a slight emphasis along the lines of religious mediation: ("Try to see things from God's point of view"). This is, in fact, the level on which Mr. Wilson is operating, as can be seen by his replies [34], [38], and [39].

Unless we are mistaken, Counselor Y's replies in the last section of this dialogue, taken with those made by Y₅ in the previous extracts, make up a harmonious combination of three fundamental attitudes: welcome, guidance, and mediation.

Summary

The analysis of this dialogue, which began as a simple request for advice, provides a vivid illustration of the difficulties encountered by the directive function in replies which are either judicative, exploratory, general, or interpretative. Not that these types of replies should be systematically outlawed from all pastoral dialogue, as is the case in certain types of psychotherapeutic relations. But we must be careful to make sure that pastoral relations are not structured (and soon paralyzed) on habitual reactions which are the long-term effect of this type of reply on a counselee: defensive hostility, passive dependence, lack of affective satisfaction, the breaking up of the relationship.

An examination of the reflective type of reply shows the advantages to be gained from it: security, a deeper motivation that is better accepted, a broader awareness of the facts of the situation, and a final decision made quite independently of all outside influences, of all third parties, and of the counselor's own opinion. Note that the "security" in question means the possibility of giving full and honest expression to opinions or states of mind. This does not necessarily make the final decision any "easier." On the contrary, many people will be much more uneasy when they fail to find a counselor who will come out loud and clear with the "right" solution. But is not this fundamental anxiety the basis of our freedom in its quest for the future? And, finally, is it not the most powerful leaven for raising the consciousness toward God, to become itself again in Him, through prayer? On these two counts, a place of honor should be reserved for such training for freedom in pastoral psychology, at the very heart of the directive function.

Directing the counselee, therefore, is not a question of merely guiding his behavior; it is not a question of providing thoughts, principles, plans, or resolutions. It is the progressive awakening of his personality and his freedom when faced with the objective values of morality and religion. Even when these are called for or when an explicit "declaration" is required in answer to a direct question concerning, for instance, remarriage after divorce—if these moral obli-

gations are to be recognized for what they are, changes will
have to be made in the person's psychological, moral, and
religious motivations. The "director's" task is to assist this
process.*

The directive function would be extremely limited and
sadly multilated if it were concerned solely with moral
debate, intellectual enlightenment, and on-the-spot advice,
even when based on excellent principles. Our attention
should penetrate beneath the counselee's words and beyond
the material content of what he is saying, to focus on the
state of his latent or expressed motivation and on the actual
potential and the limits of a freedom which must be awak-
ened to a greater awareness of itself and of God.

3   The Mediative Function

Pastoral care does not end with the psychological or
pedagogical influence of one man over another, any more
than it began as a purely human initiative. Its goal is to
substitute the work of God for the work of man. If unsuccessful, it will lapse either into psychologism (first function) or pseudopedagogical moralism (second function),
which St. Paul placed in sharp contrast with an authentic

---

* When they seek a priest's advice, Christian counselees are often perfectly (and sometimes not so perfectly) well aware of the theoretical
moral answer to their questions. So, instead of giving it to them, it would
be better to make them say it for themselves. True as this may be in
moral questions, it must be admitted that the same thing cannot be said
for doctrinal, liturgical, or ascetical matters, such as the life of prayer.
Therefore, it will occasionally be necessary to issue simple, clear, precise
instruction. It will still be true that the psychological progress of the
dialogue must be aimed at the counselee's capacities for understanding,
accepting, and putting into practice the things which the counselor, thanks
to four years of theology, finds so easy to express in theory. This brings us
back to the question of the dynamism of the pastoral relationship which
is under discussion in this chapter.

pastoral inspiration: "Yes, you may have ten thousand schoolmasters in Christ, but not more than one father" (I Cor. 4:15). The counselee's heart and mind must be infused with the spirit of Christ. Sooner or later, to a greater or lesser degree, he must be initiated to the interior, inspirational life.

The pastor cannot allow himself to be approached as a hospitable friend unless he yields to another Love. The pastor cannot play the role of an enlightened guide unless he effaces himself completely to reveal the source of another Light. "I am not the Christ; I have been sent to go before him. The bride is for the bridegroom; but the bridegroom's friend, who stands by and listens to him, rejoices too, rejoices at hearing the bridegroom's voice; and this joy is mine now in full measure. He must become more and more, I must become less and less" (John 3:28-30).

This is the common axis around which the two preceding functions revolve: the mediative function, which can be accomplished only by holding out a welcoming hand, which can be heard only when the interior voice starts to relay the speaker's words to the counselee's innermost soul.*

The psychological attitude necessary for the adequate exercise of this third function is the most difficult to describe and to maintain. Certainly, there must be constant recourse to prayer to keep the pastor in touch with the ulti-

---

* It must be emphasized that in combining the three functions, the priest is definitely acting as a mediator and not as a simple intermediary. His mission once completed, the intermediary stops work and disappears. Mediation continues after its goal has been attained. This is why Christ is known as the mediator and not the intermediary between God and man. The same is true of the work of the Church and her priests, from both a sacramental and a strictly pastoral point of view. Even in the spiritual direction of the recipients of special graces and a mystical type of enlightenment, the priest's mediatory role continues to function either as a counselor or as the representative of ecclesiastical authority.[10] Pastoral mediation is constitutive of the Church's life and future, just as sacerdotal mediation in its very nature is constitutive of the Mystical Body of Christ.

mate source of his own pastoral care and of the counselee's
spiritual growth.

On the plane of psychological dispositions, the mediative
function also seems to require:

a) An infinitely patient disposition. "God is patient"
(Eccles. 18:11). We must know how to respect our neighbor's freedom and to be patient, however long the wait
may be. "Charity is patient" (I Cor. 13:4). We must be
capable of telling the counselee that the task of his sanctification is a long-term process in answer to an interior call
from God, a process which, since the pastoral dialogue has
begun, is already under way; that progress must be meas-
ured in months and years and that it will be achieved only
through a fervent, private consent in the innermost depths
of his soul.

b) Absolute confidence in the counselee's natural and
supernatural resources. From these, enlightenment and
strength must come. All assertions and suggestions that
originate with the pastor, as opposed to the counselee,
will be nothing but erratic attempts, doomed by their very
nature to be, at the best, remotely instrumental in preparing the way for success.

c) A tendency to self-effacement, to psychological withdrawal, referring the counselee back (warmly received, of
course, and duly enlightened) to his own conscience, to his
own decision—which must mature in inviolable secrecy—
and perhaps even to his own anxiety. Many counselees are
afraid that the priest will refer them back to themselves, to
their own troubled freedom, and to God's inspiration,
which they still have difficulty in accepting with confidence. And yet, would it be good for man to avoid the
anxiety of having to make certain decisions? Would it be
right for his pastoral guide to draw a discreet veil over the
harsh reality that he must work out his salvation "in anxious
fear" (Phil. 2:12).[11]

The mediative function will be but poorly served if we
limit ourselves to the material solution of a counselee's

problem (a gift of money, intercession with a wayward husband, the referral of a neurotic to a competent therapist). Thus, in the guise of charity and services rendered (highly praiseworthy, of course, and sometimes necessary), we are passing up an opportunity for directing the counselee toward the spiritual meaning of his ordeal, or of the disease which has come into his life.

Mediation will also be endangered if we enter the pastoral dialogue prepared to depend on our own intelligence, our own experience, and even upon our own natural or supernatural inspiration, to seek within ourselves for the source of any advice or the solution of the difficulties described by the counselee. On the contrary, our entire attention should be focused on the counselee, for it is only within him that the appropriate orientations will gradually emerge and be recognized; it is from him, in a far more literal sense than the beginner might imagine, that we will receive them. Thus, by the grace of a well-conducted religious mediation, the Holy Spirit works in the very relationship itself between the pastor and the counselee.

If the pastoral relationship limited itself to acceptance and understanding, it would be no more than a psychological undertaking, and certain psychotherapeutic methods would be perfectly adequate.

If the pastoral relationship could be satisfied with indicating the path to be followed and with providing the necessary strength to pursue it, then a pedagogical or moralistic approach would assure success.

If the pastoral relationship confined itself to referring the counselee to the voice of the Spirit as heard within himself, then it would not assume human nature in a human dialogue; it would no longer bear witness to the objective values of morality and religion. In spite of its accurate but abstract exposition of the goals to be attained, it would no longer be "instrumental."

In fact, all three functions are implicit and indissociable

in pastoral work. Every pastoral relationship needs the
warmth of a psychological welcome: the pastor appears as
the representative of God. It needs the firmness of pedagogical guidance: the pastor asserts himself as the bearer
of the tidings of God. It needs the prudence of spiritual
mediation: here the pastor reveals himself as a forerunner,
anticipating the direct action of the Holy Spirit.

It is up to each one to ask himself which of these three
functions seems the most habitual, and which one does not
come easily and spontaneously. Thus each person will make
a systematic effort to acquire the technical means necessary
for restoring these three functions in his work.

There are other books that deal with characteristic situations and typical forms of pastoral dialogue. This second
chapter will at least have helped the reader to see the three
main interior attitudes, without which all techniques of
relationship and dialogue are not worth a moment's trouble.

Since the religious mediation effected by means of this
interpersonal relationship is the most delicate of the three
functions, it will be considered further and illustrated with
concrete examples in the following chapter.

CHAPTER III

Human Mediation
in Pastoral Relations

IN THIS WORLD, salvation in Christ can be achieved only through the mediation of men and through life within the ecclesial community.

"Faith is born through preaching." "He who pretends to love God without loving his brother is a liar." "Outside the Church there is no salvation." "He who hears you hears me." These are the texts which form the charter of the Mystical Body of Christ and sanctify our involvement with our neighbor and the role of the priest.

A psychopastoral problem arises whenever a counselee approaches the priest in a perspective which is not in accordance with his pastoral functions as objectively defined. In the great majority of cases, the priest finds himself involved in a relationship whose affective overtones far exceed the purely religious framework. The priest must be aware of this in order to be able to distinguish these overtones and to discuss their correct application, an application which should be inspired by pastoral goals.

The threefold dialogue relationship

We believe that the relationship with the priest can be considered as structured on three levels.*

1) Priestly acts, such as administering the sacraments, and fundamental pastoral functions—welcome, guidance, and mediation—take place on a religious and supernatural level. The psychologically mature adult enters into a relationship with a priest and freely carries on a dialogue through and beyond which he becomes united to the work of God.

When asked "What do you expect from the priest?"[1] François Mauriac declared: "The priest is the man who forgives my sins and then places the host in my mouth." Then, acknowledging he was wrong, he added: "I want him to bring God to me, not to talk about Him," as if the eucharistic bread was in itself significant without the divine Word which proclaims it.

And Paul Claudel replied: "For me, the priest is Christ's representative on earth. From him I expect life through the sacraments."

For these psychologically and religiously mature Christians, the priest is both a symbolic and an efficacious representative of God; his primary efforts must therefore be devoted to behaving "as a priest." Whatever may be the mental state of the people he is caring for, the priest may turn to other considerations only provided that he remain fully aware of this basic role. As Father Bissonier[2] so wisely insists, even the chaplain of a psychiatric clinic will not attempt to develop a relationship with primarily therapeutic goals; instead, he will try to make men respond to their fundamental vocation. This, of course, cannot run counter to the patient's current mental state.

2) On the level of personal contacts, the psychological

---

* The word "level" should be stripped of all topographic connotations; it would probably be better to speak of three modalities, or of three fields of energy.

attitudes and the social background of the two participants combine to make the relationship more complex but also more valuable. Every counselee nurtures a certain image of the priest and his role. The priest in turn reacts accordingly.

A clever beggar may deliberately "play upon" the social standing of the priest in order to win influence or favors.

A woman may find the human side of her pastor's personality far from unattractive, and she may make deliberate and repeated attempts to see him.

Here we are on the level of conscious images which can be recognized for what they are, and subsequently revealed or concealed by either or both of the participants.

These anticipative images of the priest's role can either be accepted by the counselee or imposed upon him by external social or cultural pressures.[3] They can also be greatly influenced by unconscious factors, almost completely so in the case of some religious neuroses.

3) On the psychic, affective, and for the most part unconscious level, the pastoral relationship is immediately influenced by some extremely elementary needs: security and protection; love and a sense of belonging; self-esteem and the desire for acceptance by others. It can also be affected by elemental, instinctive dispositions: fear, guilt, sexuality, aggression, and anxiety. These needs and dispositions are not normally recognized for what the are but operate under a veil of excuses and rationalizations. Also, the further they are removed from normality, the more powerful and unconscious they become.

A scrupulous woman may argue incessantly about her imagined faults, while at the same time indulging her aggressive dependence, which becomes more and more pronounced with every visit to the priest.

A constant debater seems to be seeking certitude, but revels in maintaining his opposition to an authoritative image from which he is constantly seeking to free himself.

Here we are in the realm of those unconscious forces properly known as "transferential." They can have a profound effect on the role attributed to the priest, and can project themselves forcefully into the relationship with him. Strictly speaking, the term "transference" should be used only in the latter case.

1 The Counselee's Contribution: The Image of the Priest and his Role

If we are sufficiently well aware of the counselee's attitude toward us, we will generally be able to understand the psychological significance of his faith or lack of faith, of his beliefs or his refusal to believe: that is, the meaning of his attitude toward God. But this is not all. We will also have found a means, using the role he projects onto us, of making him aware of the image of God, which is alive and striving for maturity within him.

What are these roles? They exist in almost infinite variety, as numerous as there are individual counselees.

Authority, fellowship, generosity, and competence—as well as naïve ignorance, wealth, political affiliation, or superstition—each of these roles or attributes would make a topic for discussion and could be used as a chapter heading in a handbook of applied pastoral psychology.[4]

We will now borrow a hospital chaplain's list, by no means exhaustive, but containing some of the reactions with which bedridden patients disclose the role they project onto the priest from the very first moments of their meeting. As will be seen, almost all these variations revolve around the central theme of authority; several counterfeit images emerge.

Some counterfeit images of the authoritative role
a) Almost before any words have been uttered, the chap-

lain's first visit crystallizes the patient's distrust and resentment. These feelings are rarely openly expressed, except for such gruff remarks as, "You know, I don't believe in God," or, "God can't help people like me," or not in words but in an attitude of polite indifference. For the experienced chaplain there is no possible doubt—this patient has a negative reaction to authority. For him, the chaplain symbolizes an inacceptable, frustrating, or aggravating presence. His attitude reminds the patient of earlier experiences with parents, employers, supervisors, etc. The typical reaction of this type of patient to authority is to go on strike, to beat a general retreat. The attitude maintained toward God is revealed to the chaplain.

b) The chaplain frequently provokes an authoritative image, but the reactions of other patients may vary. God is sometimes seen as a sort of universal policeman and the visiting priest as one of his inspectors who wants to know whether everything (religious observance and moral conduct) is in order. These patients react negatively, but apparently in an obedient fashion. Without waiting to be asked, they assure the priest that they are good Christians: they say their prayers, and they wouldn't harm a fly. Of course, they wish to improve. They apologize for not having done more. Quite spontaneously, their religious dialogue expresses nothing but a kind of moralism. These people often attempt to reassure themselves by expressing unmistakable feelings of guilt. The priest is seen as a strict supervisor who must be mollified or appeased or even suborned—this is achieved by constant declarations of faith, protestations of faithfully observed religious practices, and a continuous preoccupation with morality.

c) Some patients react to the priest as if he were a sort of walking Santa Claus. They ask for his time, his interest, and his promise to get something done for them. By praise and flattery they try to cajole him into obtaining certain privileges or exceptions on their behalf from the hospital's medical or administrative staffs. They may eventually ask for money, but before reaching that stage they will ask him to bring them some religious books to help them pass the time. Once again, an authoritative role devolves on the priest. Some patients are reassured, and begin to feel loved and needed the moment the priest does something for them. This reassures them and may even help them to make some declarations of hostility. These childlike creatures cannot bear the idea that there are limits to the generosity of Santa Claus and that divine omnipotence is not exclusively at their disposal.

d) Other patients, generally women, see the priest as a "father" from whom they seek emotional and spiritual security and whom they handle accordingly. He has to answer their questions, calm their doubts, dispel their apprehensions, and solve their problems. Unless the chaplain is on the alert, he will find himself invested with the full responsibility for situations and decisions which, on the strictly pastoral level, have nothing whatsoever to do with him. This particularly insidious form of dependence often succeeds because it makes the priest feel important, useful, or generous. He provides answers, gives advice, and undertakes tasks which the patient (or her family) could have done perfectly well for herself. Sometimes it is too late when the priest realizes that he has allowed himself to be manipulated, and that no sooner are the first problems solved than new ones arise.* Sometimes he also realizes that the counselee has used his advice and his replies as pre-

* We do not wish to be accused of suggesting that a priest should never perform these services or undertake certain tasks, especially when people are incapable of taking care of these things for themselves. He can—and sometimes, like any other Christian, he must—undertake different tasks in the cause of friendship, charity, or mutual aid. He may occasionally provide money, find a room, a job, and so forth. Could not these activities be considered as "parapastoral"? In any case, the danger here lies in considering a pastoral relationship as satisfactory when it is based exclusively on this type of activity.

texts for attacking and rejecting him, or that the counselee has done the exact opposite of what he advised. The latter reaction can also show that the counselee is testing the chaplain's interest in him. On the whole, therefore, this is a promising state of affairs—provided that the priest does not resent it.

e) Other people look on the priest as the harbinger of death: "You've come to see me? There's no need for that, I assure you. I'm really much better. The doctor himself told me so this morning." In fact, the priest's presence re-awakens secret conflicts, and the result is a terrible state of anxiety. Often the chaplain will discover the truth behind this interpretation, not during this first visit, but on a later occasion when the patient's anxiety has somewhat diminished.

f) There are some who see the priest as a "holy man," inhabiting another world and totally unaware of day-to-day contingencies, an idealist who has never had to face the sordid, painful facts of life. This defensive position is some-times adopted as justification for a complete refusal to have anything to do with the priest.

g) For others, the priest is someone with extraordinary powers. With no effort on their part, he will automatically renew their relationship with God by means of prayer and the sacraments. Thus, some prayer offerings are often tainted with magic rather than signed with the seal of faith.

h) Finally, a great number of counselees—and this group proliferates today—welcome the priest as a skilled coun-selor, as a sort of expert in psychology, who will help them (gratis) solve their premarital, family, financial, or even medical problems. They would be astonished, shocked even, to hear that the priest is not there for that purpose.

Perhaps this catalogue of human reactions provoked by the mere arrival of a priest in a hospital ward may help the reader to grasp the amazing variety of psychological roles which are thrust upon the priest. Yet we have only mentioned variations on the authoritative role.

Most of these processes are set in motion before the patient gets to know the chaplain, before there is any word or action on his part. They are, therefore, latent but not unconscious, like the preformed attitudes or prefigured images that condition the patient's psychological expectations. If these reactions continue after several interviews, they may very well be either the result of this prefiguration or the effect of the personality and attitude of the chaplain himself.

The reactions of the priest

In these circumstances, the psychopastoral progress of the priest depends upon: 1) his ability to perceive the variety of roles offered; 2) an awareness of his own tendency toward a blind acceptance of certain roles and an aggressive refusal of others; 3) an ability to decide how to deal with these relationships, which are not wrong in themselves, provided that they undergo a process of self-purification and that they grow to maturity like the relationship with God, of which they are a human symbol.

One fact stands out: All the preceding categories share the same limitation—it is the patient's attitude alone that is examined. From the opening words of the pastoral dialogue, this attitude will turn into a constantly developing relationship between the counselee and the priest. But the relationship will be formed by the priest's attitude and his replies, which will either develop it further or keep it at the same level. We will now re-examine the eight situations, considering them in the same order.

a) If a priest suffers from a sense of insecurity or feels impelled to assert his own prestige, he will be unable to meet the aggressive refusal. "I don't believe in God; he can't help people like me." He will merely give a wry smile, instead of accepting this as a starting point and calmly replying: "You really believe that it is so difficult to help you that even God couldn't manage it?"

b) He will accept all declarations of obedience and of conscientious religious observance at their face value, offering compliments instead of a reproof, and saying, "Of course, of course, I'm sure you are a good Christian," instead of, "So you think I'm here to check up on your religious practices?"

c) He will make promises and waste his time trying to obtain privileges instead of referring requests to the proper authorities and making sure that legitimate requests are taken care of.

d) He will agree to solve problems, saying, "If I were you, this is what I would do," instead of, "Nobody can make your decisions for you. There are arguments on both sides. Place yourself before God and make your free choice," adding perhaps, "Would you like us to say a prayer together, to help you prepare for this decision?"

e) He will say, "Perhaps you are getting better, but your condition is still serious. You must think of how you are going to spend eternity" (as if one couldn't consider it just as well while in the best of health) instead of, "I came to see you because I heard you were better. Why don't we talk about your plans for the future?" (Including eternity.)

f) He will behave like a man making announcements in the name of God instead of listening carefully and providing a genuine reaction to what is said while maintaining a steadfast belief in the mysterious saving action of God.

g) He will accept the offering, which is understood as meaning that his prayers are worth more than the patient's, instead of saying kindly, "I'll certainly remember you during my Mass, but nobody can earn your salvation for you."

h) He will transform the dialogue into a psychological consultation instead of making it clear that he is qualified to discuss psychological situations only in terms of their religious significance. He will become the person who is always on hand to calm, reassure, sooth, and anesthetize, forgetting to get at the true meaning behind the worries, conflicts, and anxieties by leading them back toward God.

Priests in need of prestige or respect will behave in this way, reciprocating the authoritative role projected upon them and the dependent attitude of certain counselees. This is extremely unfortunate, for they might very well have accepted the proposed relationship, even in its counterfeit versions, in order to reveal gradually its true nature and at the same time develop the relationship existing between themselves, the counselee, and God.

In fact, any psychological relationship established with a priest contains the necessary potential for developing a relationship with God. Many priests complain that they are unable to exercise this mediative function which is justly so dear to them. They do not know on what it should be based, what it should consist of, and when it should be used. In many cases it would be quite enough for them to go along with the counselee's obvious interpretation of their priestly role, in order to reveal the course open to him and to "launch" him on his religious voyage.

Passive dependence, superstition, and moralism—all inadequate versions of the genuine religious attitude—are brought immediately into play in the relationship between counselee and priest. Their true nature should be kindly and patiently revealed so that work can be resumed along more genuinely religious, Christian lines.

Many priests would prefer to see more of their pastoral interviews take place on a religious level. It would be extremely useful for them to begin a systematic examination of the relationship proposed by each counselee, afterwards examining its complex nature and the use to which it was put. This relationship is a vital principle of pastoral work and even of teaching. The intellectual or affective conflicts for which so many people seek assistance are all aroused or revived by significant interpersonal relationships in the course of their previous experience. Often it is not the image of God alone that we are dealing with in these conflicts, but also that of the priest. One acts as a detector for the other. Even, psychologically, while the rough outline of a dialogue is being sketched out, the priest is seen as re-presenting God. In the same way, it is through a fresh relationship with the priest that many counselees will be able to rediscover the authenticity and to consolidate the maturity of their relationship with God.

The relationship between the priest and the counselee depends on the thoughts and emotions that each is capable of expressing in front of the other. Quite apart from any question of pastoral success, the greater the priest's emotional maturity the greater will be his sense of personal security, and he will be all the more capable of recognizing and accepting, in order to rise above them, the variety of roles projected onto him by his counselees.

Unconscious needs and transference relations

However, there are problems, especially when the consciously expressed attitudes are subtended by a transference originating and operating—for the counselee at least—on a strictly unconscious level. The image of the priestly role is thus falsified within the relationship itself and is, accordingly, much more difficult to control. This role can also be correctly expressed on a verbal level, while the actual relationship itself remains unaffected. What then, exactly, is transference?

The transference theory

Transference does not mean that the counselee feels sympathy or love for the counselor, nor, on the other hand, that he adopts a consciously aggressive attitude toward him either in speech or actions. Strictly speaking, transference is an unconscious aspect of the relationship, stemming from past repressions.

In fact, the contacts between counselee and priest can be deeply structured by certain innate dispositions which are either temperamental or are acquired by the counselee in the early years of his life. Frustrations caused by his mother, fear of his father, or guilt feelings toward his brothers and sisters may have scarred him so deeply that these primordial emotional experiences are reawakened by his meeting and dialogue with the priest or other counselors. He is incapable of loving without a fear of loss, disagreeing without deep anxiety, collaborating without a sense of rivalry, or giving orders without riding roughshod over other peoples' consciences and privacy. His present relationships are the unconscious extension of past relationships which still weigh him down.

The chief characteristic of transference is a tendency to ambiguous emotions and ambivalent behavior.

For example, a counselee may be consciously expressing his complete confidence in a priest, while at the same time the relationship between them may be unconsciously developing on an affective basis of fear, built up by a repressed fear of his father, acquired during infancy. This means that in order to live in security, this man must adopt an attitude of passive dependence—hence the obedient and apprehensive manner in which he approaches the priest and perhaps even follow his advice.

Criteria

How are we to tell whether any of the established relationships display more or less acute signs of transference?

Apart from specialized training, which will presumably be of little help to him (such as a course in psychotherapy), the priest must be satisfied with very general criteria. He should be able to easily recognize the transferential character of a relationship by a particular tenacity in maintaining certain topics of conversation, by the counselee's resistance to the simplest explanation and, finally, by a certain ambiguity or ambivalence in the personal relationship, of which we have just given an example.

1) Normally the tenacity or even the strength with which certain attitudes are expressed can be extremely revealing. In spite of numerous explanations and careful, detailed summaries, the counselee keeps harping on the same subjects, repeating the same reactions, and accentuating the affective nature of his relations with the priest.

Unless a set of transference-based defenses is in operation, the man to whom the priest said, "You're probably quite right; it can't be too easy to help you," will not suddenly relapse a week later and repeat, "God can't help people like me." He will either examine his problem more closely or change the subject.

2) Resistance of any attempt made at revealing its true nature is a useful test for distinguishing a counselee's initial, conscious image of the sacerdotal role from an unconscious, tyrannic need.

The priest replies, "So you think I'm here to check up on the way you practice your religion," thus accepting the counselee's approach while simultaneously revealing the falsity of the image projected onto himself as a priest. In this case, the counselee never continues for long along these lines. Provided he is not the victim of unconscious urges and needs, he laughs and begins to speak about other things—with the priest at any rate.

Once a given threat has been revealed, it loses its significance, provided no transference exists.

3) Ambiguous or ambivalent personal contacts, especially when they occur with the resistance which has just been described, are undoubtedly the most conclusive proof of all. Every priest has met the type of person who asks for a favor while trying to give the impression that he really came for something else; who gives vent to protestations of obedience while surreptitiously unleashing vast quantities

of aggression and pride; who follows the priest's advice, but only in order to prove that the priest was wrong; who speaks of complete confidence or even an affectionate attachment for the priest, but whose behavior reveals his fear and apprehension. In these cases, the relationship remains inauthentic—a mixture of love and hate.

This sense of inauthenticity in pastoral relations can be extremely irritating when it drags on and deteriorates for weeks or months. Personally, we feel that it provides an acid test for abnormality, although the degree of gravity may vary greatly.[5]

The person is totally unaware of these affective motives underlying his apparent motivation—they are unconscious. This is why the situations just described do not call for any moral judgment from a priest who has noted their transferential significance. There is no question of hypocrisy or bad faith or duplicity. A priest with a sketchy knowledge of psychic mechanisms may show a tendency to make moral evaluations and pass judgment on the counselee. It must be emphasized that in this case, psychology will have done the priest considerable harm in his pastoral task.

Course of action

Theoretically, three courses of action are open to the counselor faced with the type of transference relationship just outlined.

1) Ignorance. The counselor fails to notice the transferential elements in the situation. Even more, he considers them as an authentic attitude of obedience, as behavior with a genuinely supernatural significance. He confuses a freely adopted moral or religious attitude toward God the Father with a psychic need for submission in the presence of an affective substitute for the counselee's own father (or mother). Worse still, without being fully aware of it, the counselor himself begins to react according to his own affective needs (for example, the urge to dominate).

2) An awareness of the relationship which is used to

make the "patient" gradually conscious of his psychic needs. A therapist may even deliberately create a situation in which the amount of transference is increased in order to facilitate its subsequent solution on the psychological level. But this is a technique proper to psychotherapy. It would seem that no priest should attempt to work along these lines unless he is explicitly qualified to do so and unless his aim becomes this psychic transformation which in itself lies outside his pastoral field.

3) This leaves an awareness of the transference and a decision to put it to religious use without attempting to make the counselee aware of it (not, at any rate, of the origin of the transference) and without immediately or directly condemning the special nature of the relationship—an attempt doomed to failure without the proper methods. For a priest, this seems to be the soundest approach.

Faced with a relationship in which he detects a transferential tendency, the spiritual counselor must do his best to put it to symbolic use, without making any attempt to condemn it or to remove it from the psychic area in which he is not qualified to work.

If a counselee, due to affective, unconscious needs, is passive and oversubmissive, his relationship with the priest must inevitably be affected. His spiritual guide, following a long-standing tradition in spiritual direction, will accept the full weight of this obedience in order to transfer its symbolic significance toward God. In short, he will work to replace a predetermined transference relationship involving submission to a human being with a genuine, freely chosen relationship of obedience to God.[6]

Most individual types of transference should be approached in the same way, once a pastoral counselor becomes aware of them and accepts their potential effects. As a general rule (which does not include seriously neurotic cases), the transference relationship can be put to pastoral use. When it is freely accepted and its symbolic value maintained, it will tend to split in two, one half (e.g.,

aggression) directed toward the priest, while the other
(submissiveness) is symbolically transferred to God.

In other cases it will be the need for security which clings
to the relationship with the priest while the latent anxiety
is transformed into that spiritual "anxious fear" which, St.
Paul tells us, provides the perfect accompaniment to our
quest for salvation (Phil. 2:12).

It will be readily admitted that it puts the priest at a
serious disadvantage if he is unwarned and unaware of the
transference factor, especially when he himself reacts unconsciously in the grips of a "countertransference"—for
example, when his rigid, authoritarian approach echoes the
submissive attitude of the counselee. The twofold nature of
the relationship within the fields of psychic and religious
forces thus becomes a source of perpetual confusion. Not
to mention the specifically moral danger, the pastoral counselor becomes incapable of acting as a pure mediator between the soul and the word of God, because the relation
between himself and the counselee is inextricably bound
up with their unconscious psychic processes. On the other
hand, although even a forewarned priest may find the
weight of the transference a heavy load to bear, by accepting it and tolerating it he will enable the counselee to play
an affectively valid role in their relationship which, by
analogy, becomes an equally valid means of salvation.

But before dealing any further with this "solution" of the
transference problem, let us see how these mistaken con-
cepts of the priest and his role may produce a "counter-
transference" within the priest himself.

2   The Counselor's Contribution: His Preferential Roles

The first section of this discussion of the transference
relationship seems perfectly acceptable as long as it was a
question of the counselee's attitudes, the counselee's image

of the priest, and the counselee's reactions to the pastoral dialogue. "Third person" psychology is always reassuring. As long as it concerns "someone else" it gives us a fine sense of security. It is now time to open up a new perspective, less reassuring perhaps, but strictly complementary.

The reader is already familiar with the idea that a pastoral interview is primarily an encounter between two persons, one of whom helps the other toward a greater understanding, acceptance, and expression of the divine presence. The psychological factors at work and the psychological events that occur are often far more important than what is actually said. Behind the purely verbal communication, beyond the exchange of problems and advice, lies a constantly mobile relationship between the counselor and the counselee. This relationship can either quicken the pastoral action and help it toward a conclusion—albeit a provisional one—or it can obstruct it and jeopardize its success. It would be wishful thinking to pretend that the art of pastoral relations can be improved and perfected by simple psychological education without taking the personality of the pastor himself into account.

In pastoral work, as in all human relations, a man's knowledge is limited to situations within his own experience. And we were using a didactic device when we isolated and examined the transference attitudes of the counselee alone. In fact, it is the relationship itself which is more or less intensely transferential. The priest's own attitude, the image he projects of his own role and of the counselee's, and his own reactions during a pastoral interview, all play a part, however variable, in the resulting transference.

Countertransference?

It has been suggested that the psychological part played by each priest's personality in the transferential aspect of the pastoral relationship should be termed "countertransference," since it can be considered a reaction to the attitude of the counselee. On further consideration, it is perhaps better to dispense with this idea of "counter-transference" and just refer to the twin aspects of the transference relationship itself, insofar as it is caused by latent psychological attitudes in the counselee as well as in the priest. In dealing with certain counselees and with particular problems, the priest also reveals long-established behavior patterns, often formed in early-childhood relationships with his parents. He lives his pastoral role in accordance with the more or less distinct psychological image he has been nurturing within himself.

Just as the pastoral work of the priest requires him to remain united with God on the religious and moral plane of free co-operation with divine grace, so it must be said that he will be able to fulfill his function as a psychological mediator only by exercising the strictest possible control over the transference aspect of his psychological relations with his counselees.

The threefold aspect of the pastoral relationship

The recognition and control of the transference factors in pastoral relations are always difficult for someone who has not learned the theoretical and practical distinction between the three levels (or fields of force) existing within the interpersonal relationship between the priest and the counselee. We now take these up again, but this time adopting the priest's own perspective on the threefold modality within his spiritual counseling relationship.

1) *The relationship as, ideally, he would wish or hope it to be,* conforming to the normative requirements of pastoral theology, the teaching of the magisterium and the legitimate, living traditions of a given sociocultural environment. We have already discussed the three essential functions of pastoral relations: welcome, guidance, and mediation. Normally—and even non-Christian psychologists have con-

firmed this observation—those seminarians who persevere through ordination can be distinguished by certain distinctive characteristics: openness toward other people and respect for them, disinterestedness, and generosity. These qualities help prepare and foreshadow, on the level of ordinary human relations, the operation of that divine charity which these priests strive both to represent and exercise in every encounter undertaken in God's name.

2) *The relationship as psychologically desired and consciously lived by the priest.* Not only is it true that the working of the three pastoral functions is affected by the innate gifts, character, and interests of each individual, but the image each person has of his role is inevitably shaped by innumerable familial, cultural, and social influences which structure his personality.

Why I Became a Priest is a Spanish survey initiated by the review *Seminarios* (Ediciones Sigueme, 2 vols., Salamanca, Spain), in which priests from many countries (from Cardinal Lercaro to Father Duval) explain how they see their role in the modern world. Beneath the theological constants lies the wide range of human significance which the priests see in their work.

When taking part in working groups or seminars in pastoral psychology, it is amazing to see how many different individual reactions a counselee may provoke. Needs, desires, and expectations are attributed to him in a manner which is often far from being objective. It is also amazing to see the wide range of preferential roles as selected by priests in apostolic work and to observe the way in which these are projected on both the physical and psychological levels. These images of his role which each priest projects are extremely important—unless they are recognized and discussed, it will scarcely be possible to evaluate and, if necessary, improve the quality of his pastoral dialogue.

We have often suggested the following classic situation to the members of a pastoral psychology group: a woman who has been deeply distressed by the loss of a loved one comes to see the priest and gives full rein to her revolt against God, her sinful conduct, and her intellectual doubts. After a few introductory words, each member of the group is asked to say how he would conduct such a conversation.

If a sufficiently tolerant, friendly atmosphere prevails in the group, the variety of roles consciously and spontaneously adopted by each member soon becomes clear. One person will make a special effort to understand, welcome, comfort, and pacify. Another concentrates on attempting to enlighten and convince, to influence and guide. Another follows the same course, but shows a tendency toward moral obligations, reprimands, and the awakening of responsibility. Yet a fourth will remain so subdued and reticent that his spiritual mediation may never have any effect on his counselees unless they belong to a select few. Yet all of them, we assume, wish to bring the Glad Tidings and the grace of God to this woman in the terrible loss she has suffered and in the psychological struggle in which she is involved.

Certainly, none of the roles which each priest proposes to play is unworthy of his pastoral task. The question to be asked is: Why did this one show a preference for one particular role? What for, or, to be more exact, *who* for? Because of the needs of the counselee? If this is so, well and good. If the counselee really needs reassurance, the priest should reassure her. If she needs to be shaken up a little the priest should admonish her. If she needs advice, the priest should be a firm, persuasive guide—always bearing in mind the constant goal of any pastoral relationship: the sanctification of a human soul.*

---

* Here group work seems to be almost indispensable. As he listens to other priests reacting in different ways to the same situation, each priest begins to examine the nature of his own initial reaction and, of his own accord, he begins a discreet re-evaluation of his own role as he understands it, always bearing in mind the wide variety of his counselees' possible needs.

But are not these different roles sometimes adopted almost automatically because they meet the priest's own
needs? This is true, for instance, when the priest himself
experiences a sense of security as he offers reassurance, of
power whenever he displays a certain degree of severity, of
serenity when he gives advice, or of generosity when he
provides help for someone who turns to him for temporal
assistance. And if the priest's own needs remain unsatisfied
even to a small degree, won't he then begin to play a role
in front of many, if not all, of his counselees? Unless he
acts as counselor, adviser, teacher, or leader, he no longer
feels that he is achieving pastoral success.

But even if this is the case, if the role assumed by the
priest corresponds largely or even uniquely to his own
needs, the pastoral relationship need not lose all value, because this sort of help might be exactly what the counselee
requires. However, the priest is setting out on a downward,
increasingly narrowing path: he is gradually reducing the
range of his psychological keyboard. He has a tendency to
play the same notes over and over again, the notes which
he himself enjoys hearing—whatever the state of mind or
the counselee's "musical ear" may be. And since he enjoys
his own performance, it is often difficult for him to realize
that his pastoral work has become *dis*-cordant in the most
literal sense of the word: it is no longer in harmony with
the real needs of his counselees, or, at least, of the majority
of them.

When this evolutionary process is complete, the pastoral
duties with which the priest is charged may give him an
opportunity of creating his own public. By a more or less
conscious process of selection, he manages to meet more
and more persons of the same type, the type he can help
(sometimes very effectively) without abandoning the nar-
row role in which he himself finds security and satisfaction.
Although he lives under the impression that he is enjoying
enormous pastoral success, he will, in fact, have created a
closed world for himself, fulfilling his own needs. His func-

tion as a religious mediator will now be even more seriously
hampered by his abandonment of the struggle to maintain
or restore the whole range of psychological roles which
should be at his disposal, not geared to his own needs but
based on the honestly observed needs of his counselee—
transitory as these needs may often be. In this affective
partnership which develops between the priest and his own
specially selected public, any psychological progress toward
transcendence becomes increasingly unlikely. However successful the pastoral dialogue may be in psychological or
human terms, it no longer produces that opening up to God
which should provide as great an incentive for the counselee as it does for the priest himself.

3) *The relationship as it emerges without the priest's becoming aware of it,* probably shrouded in a mass of justifica-
tions and a thousand rationalizations, based on a defense
reflex and a psychological need for a "clear conscience."
We are now in the field of unconscious and mainly transferential motivations.

On the psychic level, the attitude adopted by the priest
toward other people is no different from that of any other
person at the beginning of a relationship. Even for the
priest, pastoral relations echo and reflect a set of basic emotional drives, including security, a need for success and self-
esteem, a desire to be accepted and loved by others, a tendency to protect, influence, and dominate others; or certain
affective predispositions: fear, sexuality, aggression, anxiety,
guilt, etc. These aspirations and affective predispositions
are not always recognized for what they are.* And is it
always advisable that they should be? In any case, the priest

---

* It is even more difficult to recognize them when dealing with priests
or nuns who have received a thorough intellectual training: they are so
inclined to rationalize, producing involved excuses which always seem to
explain their behavior either as a form of sublimation or as based on
spiritual motives.

should become aware of them when they begin to interfere with the conscious pursuit of his pastoral role (which we have been studying in earlier sections) and when there is a risk of possible damage to the mediatory function itself.

One priest will undertake apostolic work only among men. According to him, it is much too easy to waste time working with women—and they are so fickle! He is sixty-five. How can anyone expect him to recognize here the final hardening of an attitude acquired at the age of sixteen as a result of an adolescent disappointment with one of his teen-age friends?

Another priest feels at ease only among children. He has a lively personality and is a brilliantly talented storyteller. According to him, the whole world could be won over within one generation if all young people could be Christianized. But after listening in to some of his lessons, we begin to get the idea that this man has a problem closely linked to the exercise of authority and psychological domination. Only the world of children can offer him the captive, attentive, and emotionally submissive audience that he needs. His father dominated him as a child, and now the priest adopts the same attitude toward the children he is now teaching. Moreover, as far as the children are concerned, the priest makes no attempt to listen to them or to get to know them. He is quite happy just to talk to them.

In the rough outline we have given of these two situations, we are confronted with the unconscious forces which constitute the personalities of these two priests. As far as their consciously projected roles are concerned, we could speak about a narrowing of their apostolic range. But as long as their compulsions (antifeminism and a desire to dominate a group of children) remain unconscious, we will witness a gradual deterioration of their apostolate, even among the men and children with whom they enjoy working. Generally speaking, it is hopeless to attempt to establish pastoral relations with men unless one is capable of meeting their womenfolk as well. And the "transferential" authority exercised over children generally involves anti-educative attitudes which do little to advance human or religious development.

Once again—but this time on the part of the priest—the two special characteristics of a transference relationship are recognizable: a pronounced distortion in the perception of other people and in behavior toward them and the early origin of this distortion, harking back to childhood, or adolescent situations in which the broad outline of their personality structure may be found.

General tendencies to transference

There are certain general symptoms and personal features which may lead one to suspect the existence of trans-ferential tendencies in priests. These will now be analyzed in greater detail.

1   THE SPONTANEOUS ACCEPTANCE
OR REFUSAL OF CERTAIN ROLES

This has already been discussed in the previous section concerning the priest and the roles he assumes. There is probably some unconscious motivation at work whenever you find a particular tenacity, exclusivity, or lack of authenticity in the use made of one of the following roles. This may take the form of a preferential choice or an outright refusal.

The authoritative role, which often reciprocates the attitude adopted by many counselees and is partially connected to the pastoral function itself. This role may also be refused by other priests who can feel comfortable only in an "all pals together" type of relationship, using nothing but a friendly "good child" approach which, they believe, will relieve them of exercising an authority whose weight is sometimes hard to bear.

The role of moral and spiritual counselor, so often sought after today by so many of the faithful who tend to reduce it to the level of simple psychological assistance. A role which may also be refused by other priests who are opposed to the psychological improvement of pastoral relationships and who resist anything tending to call their own personality into question.

The role of mediator, the man inclined to withdraw in favor of a closer contact between the soul and God on the spiritual plane or in favor of referral to the appropriate specialists (psychologists, psychiatrists, or social workers) who are better qualified to solve certain specific problems. This role of humble mediator can also be completely rejected or only occasionally accepted by other priests who obscure the issue for themselves with talk of laxism or illuminism on the spiritual plane and of the lack of moral and religious values supposedly inherent in a certain course of treatment, even when administered by specialists guaranteeing a maximum degree of reliability and security.

The continuous acceptance or constant refusal of any one of these psychological functions in pastoral work is tantamount to expressing a lack of maturity, leading one to suspect the existence of transference tendencies. It is impossible to discuss the real nature or the origin of these tendencies without exploring an individual's personal background. Little progress will be made as long as one expects to combat these sterile attitudes by the simple diffusion of psychological knowledge, however relevant it may be. This type of progress demands the constant supervision of pastoral work by a qualified psychologist, or a sense of awareness gained from participation in working groups organized for this purpose.

2 EXCESSIVE EMOTIONAL INVOLVEMENT
   OR THE LACK OF IT

Granted that the pastoral relationship is not primarily an exchange of ideas but an interpersonal meeting, the style of this meeting may be influenced by the priest's own emotional needs or affective defenses, which may run in two directions:

a) Excessive emotional involvement. One priest is happy only when he is doing work in which he can share the emotional life of the people who turn to him. His priestly words and actions will not be judged according to their objective success but by the quality of the disclosures made and the emotional reactions which he both observes and provokes. Provided people confide in him, all will be well. There is confusion here between exercising influence, having confidence, and enjoying someone's confidence. Many priests and teachers have influenced people who had little confidence in them and who certainly never took them into their confidence. Other priests enjoy people's confidence without ever sharing any confidential intimacies. But the priest under discussion here will not rest until he has provoked exchanges of a sentimental or vaguely confidential nature. Without these, his work seems dull and unsatisfactory.

Some priests are often extremely shy, highly emotional, and quick to identify themselves with a certain type of counselee. They are deeply marked by infantile frustrations, and there may well be some slight physical handicap. They are guaranteed an audience whose members are marked by the sign of frustration. This type of counselee is never lacking among the followers of any priest. Besides, this is an honor for the priesthood, which should be prepared to relieve all forms of distress—even psychic ones—in the name of God.

In the worst cases, the pattern of a vaguely sentimental relationship can be seen emerging; this may involve real moral danger, especially when women in need of affective support are involved.

At best there is a marked restraint among those people— men especially—for whom the priest might have acted as a religious mediator. Also, any spiritual aid provided is usually linked to the permanence of the psychological relationship. The departure of this type of priest immediately plunges his "flock" into the darkest gloom and despondency.

b) Refusal of all emotional involvement. On the other hand, a priest may have developed—almost without being aware of it—a particular style which he adopts in meetings and conversations, from which any hint of affective involvement is rigorously excluded: a cold, correct welcome; rigidly moralistic advice, highly intellectualized personal exchanges.

Excellent as they may be for the clarity of their thought and their clear-cut advice, these priests often succeed in rebuffing a large number of counselees whom they might very well have been able to reach in return for a slightly greater degree of personal involvement. Unfortunately, insecurity has left too deep a mark on them. Without really intending it and without being aware of it, they withdraw from any genuine human relations.

This is often the case with mild sexual obsessives whose personal equilibrium has been maintained only by means of extensive repression. In the worst cases, they are cold, unhappy, schizoid* personalities whose religious relations, valid as they may be as far as personal sanctity is concerned, are never based on that foundation of human sympathy which is essential for all laborers in human society. Can personal sanctity compensate for this deficiency? Can it, with the help of the grace of the priesthood, transform this

---

* "Schizoid" is a term applied to people with a reduced sense of affective awareness of the everyday world and especially of the people living in it. Objects and people are perceived, not as themselves, but in relation to the subjective, egocentric needs of the individual. It should be noted that this is diametrically opposed to the contemplative approach in which a person is united to an object in an entirely gratuitous manner by complete psychological self-absorption in it.

fundamental, psychic penury? The answer is that, of course, it can, but whether it normally does so seems extremely doubtful.

3 The Meaning of the Counselor's Choice of Certain Types of Counselee

Certain processes of selection or rejection regularly employed by priests in the "creation of their own public" often seem to be based on unconscious, transferential motivations. Pastoral work among the elderly, among women, among the managerial classes, or among intellectuals often lends itself to the revival of unconscious structures.[7]

We will discuss only the first example: the difference in age.

Old people

Sometimes a difference in age can create problems which are quite unconnected with the obvious objective difficulties of understanding, helping, or even taking an interest in these people when they turn to us for assistance.

For many people, the attitudes which their own parents or grandparents aroused in them will be unconsciously revived in the presence of elderly persons. Thus a priest who suffered a strained and painful relationship with his own mother may encounter unusual difficulty in giving pastoral assistance to elderly women, and may also observe a tendency in himself to make fun of them at every opportunity—in their absence. If it was the relationship with his father that was difficult, the same negative transference can take place with elderly men. This diagnosis is especially obvious when the external or internal aggressive tendencies are directed exclusively toward elderly men *or* elderly women.

On the other hand, many elderly people arouse protective or paternalistic instincts: a priest with pronounced supervisory or directive tendencies or with an urge to deal with the emotivity of others may, while enjoying great success among the elderly, actually exercise a paralyzing influence or induce the revival of infantile attitudes during the final years of these old people's spiritual life.

Besides, the idea that these old people have already finished their lives, that they have become rigid and unapproachable, serves as a justification for a cynical or indifferent attitude toward them.

However, many spiritual relationships with old people can result in extraordinary spiritual growth. Is not this the period when many impart an ultimate significance to their life? People often fail to observe that there are certain natural dispositions in psychobiological aging which tend to produce detachment, resignation, and a Christian acceptance of death.[8]

Recognizing transference tendencies in oneself

It might be advisable to examine one's conscience from time to time concerning these three types of general symptoms. But apart from these, there are certain classic signs, readily observable in everyday life, which might well become the objects of a regular psychopastoral examination of conscience.

The fifteen warning signals which follow have been selected in pastoral psychology seminars and in individual supervisions as being the most frequent and the most useful. Every one of us has probably displayed at least one of them in the course of pastoral work with certain people.

A PSYCHOPASTORAL
EXAMINATION OF CONSCIENCE

I should suspect myself of displaying a tendency toward the transferential aspect of a counselor-counselee relationship if I—

feel uneasy, sad, or depressed or, on the contrary, elated, enthusiastic, or excited about the counselee;

experience sudden waves of enthusiasm or boredom during our meetings;

have long, impassioned arguments with him;

feel worried by his reproaches or his criticism;

derive enormous conscious pleasure from his congratula-
tions, his signs of satisfaction, gratitude, or affection;

am incapable of refusing to adopt the expected attitude
(e.g., reassurance, praise, encouragement, friendship);

steer the conversation away from certain subjects which
he brings up (e.g., death, sexual experience, money);

maintain a continuous dependence in the counseling relationship, especially by the constant use of reassuring
words and phrases;

encourage the counselee in his aggressive self-release from
a relationship against which he is rebelling, e.g., against
his family, his wife, or his employer;

feel obliged to help him by interfering in the details of
his daily life, by taking the initiative in his place (e.g.,
telephoning the doctor) or by easily resolving problems by the use of personal influence;

am careless about the practical details of our meetings,
or take unusual pains over them (e.g., punctuality,
choice of room, arrangements for the next meeting);

make a point of discussing his case with my colleague,
emphasizing his importance, his merits, or his personality;

talk about him in an ironic or cynical manner;

worry continually about the successful outcome of his
case, about whether he is following my advice, and
about keeping in contact with him;

dream about the counselee.

If three or four of these fifteen items figure in our relations with the same counselee, the chances are good that
our own personal problems are interfering with his problems in the course of our pastoral dialogue. There is noth-

ing disastrous about this, nothing that will necessarily ruin our pastoral efforts on his behalf, provided that we are fully aware of the situation and that we are determined to control its transferential elements, thus avoiding one of those "affective partnerships" which lead our mediatory function down paths leading to a religious dead end.

3 The Pastoral Resolution of Transference

In his pastoral dialogue, as in the rest of his existence, the priest has no other ambition than to become that unsullied mediator, "the man of God." Unfortunately, except for his sacramental gestures and the supernatural exercise or a mediation rendered effective by God alone on the level of faith, he can only struggle along on a psychological level toward this ideal relationship. Personal sanctity will not suffice: his personal example and his counseling often fall far below the level of his own religious life.

Psychologically speaking, pastoral relations often emerge weighed down by the conscious or unconscious affective needs of the pastor and the counselee. Clearer thinking would reveal the enormous gap between what one hopes to do and what is actually achieved. The dispelling of a few illusions need not necessarily involve the slightest discouragement, provided that 1) we increase our trust in a strictly salutary action, the work of God alone. This supernaturally effective action is achieved by means of the most unworthy mediations without ever being intrinsically dependent upon them. Psychopastoral work has but one "dispositive" aim, which is to prepare the ground for the work of grace; 2) we must remain faithful to the call of charity, which urges us to seek all available means for improving the quality and the flexibility of our pastoral relations, consistent with that supernatural mediation, the sole basis of our entire faith.

Moreover, this psychopastoral examination of conscience is not empty practice. By examining past relationships, it looks forward to dialogues to come. By clearly revealing the underlying affective predispositions in pastoral work, psychology collaborates very closely with it in observing their development and, if necessary, in correcting them. Even if this reveals the structure of certain "affective partnerships" and their deleterious effect on pastoral relations, the means for their correction generally emerges at the same time.[9]

Religious mediation and transference

Transference in itself is not so much an obstacle as a means to an end. The establishment of a transference-based relationship no more impedes the development of sound pastoral practice than infantile anthropomorphism prevents the adolescent or adult from eventually attaining a purified—or even mystical—theocentric faith.

a) The passive dependent approaches the priest in search of authoritative, or at least authorized, pronouncements to allay his own anxiety, and to see to it that he will not have to face God on his own.

b) The timid, frustrated type, eager for affection, will begin a dialogue in the hope that the priest will provide a risk-free love and the illusion that the counselee has yielded himself up to God without any real obligation or effort on his part.

c) The scrupulous man, urged on by an imaginary guilt, will cling pitilessly to the man of God, fiercely tormenting him, while he himself dons the masks of suffering.

This is but the beginning. The mere appearance of transference in pastoral dialogue is unimportant. What counts is that the counselor be aware of it and know how to deal with it. In any case, like it or not, each of these relationships will have its own case history. In describing this case history and studying the possible outcome of each of these "typical" relationships, we will be able to sketch in the main lines of a pastoral psychology which will be quite different from any therapeutic psychology. In the present state of our knowledge, we can attempt only a very rough outline.

In the third section of this chapter we will try to show how a pastoral relationship, even when based on effective transference, can gradually transform itself and even "resolve" itself into an authentic attitude toward God as well as toward the priest.[10]

The development of transference relationships

The transference relationship is an opening, initial fact, but it can become a means. The true pastoral relationship consists of a work to be done and continually perfected, on the plane of freedom with the enlightenment of grace.

In the course of a prolonged, regular, or intermittent course of spiritual direction, three possible lines of development emerge.

First case: transference
remains unconscious for both parties . . . .

Neither the priest nor the counselee seems properly aware that the strength of the bond which has formed between them does not depend upon anything that has been said, nor on the priest's known religious function, but on the mutuality of affective roles they are constantly exchanging.

a) In response to the need for passive dependence comes the priest's satisfaction at being able to play an authoritative role.

b) In response to a need for affectionate understanding comes the joy at being able to provide a little consolatory warmth, under the impression that this is the same as charity.

c) In response to obsessive self-justification by a flood of useless, sterile self-accusations comes the infinite patience which, to some people, is the mark of greatness in the pastoral treatment of the scrupulous.

Under these conditions, any maturation of the transference relationship remains highly improbable. As long as both parties remain unaware of the affective situation, and unless one of them decides to take the affective aspect in hand, bringing it to light in order to reduce or resolve it, the pastoral relationship will simply mark time—not, of course, on the supernatural plane, where the merits of both parties may be great, but on the psychological plane.

Not to mention the gross inconvenience caused by the waste of time, exchanges of gifts, and the serious risk of an affective drift toward less worthy behavior, there is sure to be a sense of stagnation and, in the long run, disgust at these useless, uneventful conversations. This can scarcely be described as the evolution of a relationship but as its gradual exhaustion.

Second case: the counselee
   becomes aware of transference
   Certain external events—marriage, maternity, moving to a new home or job, and psychological treatment—may produce a maturation, or at least a transformation, of the transference, simply by raising it to a conscious level. This often happens when persons who have grown accustomed to spiritual direction start or conclude therapeutic treatment. These people often sever relations with their old spiritual director, who almost inevitably reacts with caustic criticism about the psychotherapist. This particular situation is probably largely responsible for the misunderstandings that exist between priests and psychotherapists.

In fact, all this is perfectly normal. The maturation of the counselee, especially when it is accelerated as in psychotherapy, produces a whole series of "reconsiderations." Many previous relationships and present habits will now seem, rightly or wrongly, to be due to affective or even neurotic tendencies which he is now outgrowing or attempting to remedy. His concept of the people and events in the external world undergoes a profound change. Even his ideas concerning religion and the priest are affected. The critical period through which he is now passing is the price to be paid for this accelerated maturation; it tends to upset relations with his spiritual director, especially if these involved any hint of transference. Moreover, the relationship which he has just established with his therapist (especially if it is a psychotherapist) immediately siphons off a large proportion of the affective urgency and energy which formerly was directed toward the priest during their spiritual meetings.

In this case, transference is dissolved and the pastoral relationship is broken.

True, there is no immediate threat to the religious future of the counselee. But the excessively psychological basis of his relationship with the priest-counselor has now been greatly modified. After all, the choice of a spiritual director depends, legitimately enough, upon certain temperamental or spiritual affinities and, normally, upon a mixture of the two. The logical outcome of a modification in these affinities is the possibility of a permanent abandonment of the spiritual director or even the temporary abandonment of spiritual direction. One often sees a gradually maturing person choosing another spiritual director who is more suited to the role expected of the priest to whom he now turns for quite different reasons and with drastically modified attitudes.

In such a case, every spiritual director, even if he cannot understand what is happening, should at least have the grace to withdraw humbly, without too great a display of ill-feeling. In fact, this would be an opportune moment to remind oneself that no one, except our Lord Himself, is indispensable for the salvation of any one of our human brethren.

Third case: the priest becomes aware
of the transferential aspect of a pastoral relationship

He attempts to check it, to "resolve" it, and to restore the full religious meaning to his psychological mediation.

This third possibility is the one to be considered as normative. Would that it occurred more frequently in pastoral work! Here a few observations are called for which may help the priest to deal with the transference situation (which often provokes unnecessary fear) and which will emphasize the difference between pastoral work and psychotherapeutic technique.

1. Transference is generally reduced when meetings between priest and counselee become fewer, shorter, and are confined to a prearranged schedule. A refusal to increase the number of sessions; a refusal to allow meetings other than those scheduled—this is the first, purely external, method for reducing affective inflation and restoring a "functional" character to the pastoral relationship (in which a man is consulted in the name of God), which it was beginning to lose.

Contrary to psychotherapeutic practice, in which attempts are sometimes made to increase transference in order to correct it at its source,[11] the priest as a religious mediator would be at fault if he deliberately attempted to increase the affective forces at play in relations between himself and his counselees. It will certainly not help in the right development of his counselees, although it may occasionally provide an easy way out. This is why he should always attempt to confine transference within the strictest possible bounds, should it appear of its own accord.

2. Transference loses its effect if it is made the explicit subject of a conversation instead of being reinforced by complementary attitudes. The spiritual director, while welcoming the counselee for what he is, should not hesitate to refuse some expected gratifications. Bearing this in mind, he should have no hesitation in making remarks extending beyond the actual conversation and concerning the quality of the relationship itself, thus forcing the counselee to become aware of the affective nuances in their relationship. The best way of dealing with them is to mention them.

The tone used must never be reproachful. It should be a simple statement or a question which they arrive at together. The mere mention of a situation is enough to bring it into the open and often to guide it toward true maturity.

a) Choosing an opportune moment, he should remark to the passive dependent: "You really seem to be in favor of any solution, provided it comes from me." Or, more succinctly, "Really, you make me want to settle all your problems for you in your place."

b) To the person with an affective attachment he should say: "Do you not feel that your visits and your problems are becoming more and more frequent simply so that you may have the pleasure of discussing them with me?" Or, should it be necessary: "Correct me if I'm wrong, but don't you come to see me whenever your husband (or your therapist) is away?"

c) With the scrupulous person and his masks of suffering, the priest should draw attention to "the strange idea you have of God. You must really bear an enormous grudge against Him to image that He could really be this way." Or: "Don't you think that by carrying on these interminable conversations as if it were you that was a victim, we are in fact getting further and further away from the truth? Above all else, you seem extremely aggressive and afraid that the secret might leak out."

It should be noted that this type of reply—

1. should never be used unless the context makes the situation absolutely clear for the priest and the remark acceptable to the counselee.

2. should never be an interpretation but a simple explanatory reflection, clarifying the content of the interview on an active plane.

Following a correctly handled transference, the therapist may find himself drawn toward an interpretation, that is, strictly speaking, the connection of present affectivity to past experiences, sometimes even going as far back as early childhood. But the priest has no need to return to the distant past, and, in any case, he lacks the necessary skill to do so. He confines himself to mentioning certain peculiarities of the actual situation, with a twofold purpose: to bring certain hitherto unperceived elements to light, and to achieve a greater authenticity by ensuring their division into a correct aim in relation to God and correct behavior in the relationship with the priest. This will be explained shortly and then illustrated with examples.

3. A transference relationship will be "resolved" in the proper sense of the term (breaking a composite down into its simplest components or parts) by a process of allowing the counselee, spiritually speaking, to carry forward to God some of his psychic attitudes to the priest, or to deflect onto the priest, symbolically or in fact, his mistaken attitude toward God.

This is true of the need for dependence, moral support, or purification—here limiting ourselves to the three "typical" cases mentioned earlier. As long as these transference impulses are directed toward a man, they must inevitably remain ambiguous and ambivalent.

a) Beneath the insidious flattery of passive dependence lurks certain aggression toward anyone attempting to retard its growth.

b) Beneath the sly words of frustration hides the terrible fear of being abandoned and unloved.

c) Beneath scrupulous complaint, the voice of an unconscious quest for vengeance can be heard and resentment against the destiny which has made it what it is.

Now, in the course of our joyful pilgrimage toward God, it is perfectly fitting for us to sometimes feel dependent, insecure ("You must work to earn your salvation in anxious fear"), unworthy, or guilty, like a child. But as long as these interior dispositions are directed toward other men, even toward priests, they will not have the authenticity of maturity and will not have attained their ultimate subject.

This applies to the fear of being judged, reprimanded, or punished, as much as to the demand for a person's presence, for his continual intervention, for security, forgiveness, etc. All these basically instinctive urges may revolve around an infantile image of God, operating solely on a perceptive level. They can also acquire a profoundly religious and spiritual significance, provided they are not diverted onto the priest and are not lived confusedly and affectively (not symbolically) in relations with him—the hallmark of an "unresolved" transference.

It is the priest's prerogative to reveal and to bring out the ultimate spiritual significance of affective urges which may well be directed at himself.

Conversely, a psychotherapist would be exceeding his mandate—or, at any rate, would seriously impair his psychotherapeutic functions—if he attempted to put the realities of the religious universe to this sort of use with his patients. He must assume a share of the transference load, but *only* in order to explain it and to cure it. It would only increase the confusion if he appeared to sanction the religious significance of a psychic disposition which, as far as his client is concerned, he should be attempting to remold.[12]

Thus the pastoral development of a transference-based spiritual relationship (always assuming that the penitent is not a neurotic, in the proper sense of the term, or that his cure seems to be temporarily out of the question) appears as follows: An ambiguous relationship with the priest is temporarily accepted and then gradually clarified; the priest then plays an active role in steering certain transferential elements onto a symbolic course, one "symbolizing" certain aspects of the mystery of salvation and of relations with a transcendent God our Saviour. These aspects of the relationship will emerge as inauthentic, provided they remain fixations of the relationship with the priest.

In this progressive development, embracing both intellectual clarification and emotional readjustment, the priest regains his role of religious mediator. After being an apparent obstacle, transference now becomes a developing agent and a tool. To quote a happy phrase of Father R. Thibaut concerning Christ, we would willingly concur that the priest, "a veiled symbol, is transformed into a symbolic veil."[13]

THREE CONCRETE APPROACHES

The following summaries of three reports, designed to trace the development of long-term pastoral work, will show just how much "progress" and how much "scission" the affective transference is capable of when it is kept under control and within strict pastoral limits. Although the reports have been considerably shortened, the main aspects of the initial meetings have been retained. The transfertial tendencies of the counselee stand out particularly well, because the priest has not yet had an opportunity of making himself known, and any image of him which may be projected is the result of largely subjective expectations.

A.   *The development of passive dependency*
A twenty-eight-year-old curate describes his relations with a young man of twenty-two who is currently doing his military service.*

THE FIRST VISIT
The boy is an extremely timid, obviously dependent personality. I answer his knock in a normal voice, but he waits outside. I have to shout two or three times. Then when he

* The actual details of these cases are either fictitious or substantially altered. As for the situational relations between the participants in the dialogue, they have been divided and rearranged in such a way that any resemblance to living persons becomes entirely coincidental.

does come in, he remains standing. I have to ask him to come forward and take a seat. He never removes his top-coat unless specifically asked to do so. Thus, before I have hardly opened my mouth, an authoritative role is thrust upon me. He asks my permission for everything. As far as he is concerned, this is all mainly unconscious. It is second nature to him. Any other behavior in my presence would seem quite out of place.

As he understands his problems, they revolve around his adjustment to army life: the discovery of certain aspects of sexuality; masturbation, which has become obsessive; the contrast between traditional family piety and barrack-room humor; a fear of girls, good or bad; an impression that relations with a "spiritual director" might help him to pull himself together. He is prepared to do anything I say, provided I tell him myself. In the course of two visits, he has found four opportunities to ask, almost pleadingly: "But what do you think I *ought* to do? In my place, what would you do?"

The young man is an only child. He lost his father when he was six, and was extremely spoiled by his mother. Thanks to her sacrifices, he was able to continue his technical studies.

ATTITUDE ADOPTED

First, obviously, the young man must be put at ease. Accept him for what he is. There should be a categorical refusal to play the transference game. Therefore, a strict decision never to discuss what he *should* do but only what he *could* do. If possible, let him find out for himself that there are several solutions to the minor problems he presents and that he must make his own choice between them.

According to what I learned in a pastoral psychology group, I am convinced that this young man's meek, dependent attitude probably conceals a latent hostility that is ripe for expression. So I shall have to refuse to do anything

which would accentuate the authoritative aspect of my role
and, by refusing to give him what he asks for (he wants me
to run his life for him), I should have no difficulty in
gradually arousing his impatience and later on his open dis-
content with what he will much later refer to as my non-
interventionist policy, my "neutral" attitude and, finally,
my "bourgeois personality."

THE CRITICAL PERIOD (SEVEN MONTHS LATER)
    In sexual matters, the young man seems close to laxism.
He is rebelling against everything he has ever been taught.
He adopts a free and easy attitude and seems to come
to see me out of pure friendliness. He never hesitates to
point out that he gets almost nothing out of our talks.

FINAL RESULT (TWO YEARS AND A DOZEN VISITS LATER)
    The young man is engaged. The girl is slightly older but
extremely feminine. They enjoy each other's company.
They discuss the future together, and it is not the girl's
suggestions that are always accepted. When he comes to
see me, he no longer asks permission to smoke. He offers
me cigarettes which I am careful not to refuse. His image
of God has greatly evolved: now God is love and a guaranty
of conjugal bliss. Shortly after he began to date the girl,
masturbation ceased almost completely.
    To my mind, his evolution seems adequate though
incomplete. He feels slightly apprehensive about being
impotent on his wedding night, the legacy of some late-
adolescent episodes in which he thinks he detects a threat
of homosexuality. He gives the impression of addressing me
as a man speaking to another man who happens to be a
priest. Both of us are striving, in the presence of God, to
cast a brighter light on questions which are no longer unimportant, but on problems concerning life as a whole or
the true significance of his actions.

CONCLUSION

It seems to me that this young man used our relationship to free himself from his passive dependence as he began to "work out"—even on me—that latent aggression which his education had repressed within him for so long. This purified his image of God, helping him to avoid sexual scrupulosity, to stop shrinking from barrack-room life and avoiding the company of young girls. He dared to lose his temper with me, thus acquiring a love-orientated image of God. As they said in the pastoral-psychology seminar: there was strong "transference scission"; his aggression was sometimes a little tiresome, but I put up with it. The result was this flowering of his capacity for love as polarized in reality on the girl and upon God as the ultimate goal of his life.

B. *The growth of an attachment rooted in frustration*

Next we have a thirty-two-year-old Sister of Charity who came for help to the priest-director of a medicopsychological counseling bureau. She was suffering from frequent fits of weeping and a sense of discouragement and despair; from utter spiritual and moral despondency; from petty impulses or thoughts of suicide. Her medical record revealed a history of asthma, dizzy spells, and revulsion against food. Her weight was down to 110 pounds, and her insomnia remained unaffected by the sleeping pills which the convent nurse had been doling out in vast quantities without worrying about the psychological aspects of the problem.

EARLY VISITS

The first impression is one of immense good will about to collapse under intolerable distress. A pronounced need to talk and eagerness to feel understood, supported, encouraged, and loved.

She comes from a large family, where generosity was the rule—to forget about yourself and give to others, to guests

or to the poor. Any display of emotion was frowned upon
and considered a sinful weakness.

Her father died when she was nine. She seems to have
been his favorite child and she remembers him as a fairly
liberal man but rather cold and a martinet for religious
observance. All six children had to go to religious festivals,
and on Sundays, family life revolved around high mass and
vespers. The portrait she paints of her mother is that of a
demanding personality, constantly urging her daughter on
to greater efforts in school and comparing her, to her disadvantage, with her brothers and sisters. Consequently, she
feels inept and incapable of achieving anything—in fact,
she had to drop out of school. However, her decision to
enter the novitiate rapidly restored her prestige within the
family.

Her novitiate passed without incident. As she was to later
remark, she was "as good as gold." She was living a con-
tinuation of her family life at home and she was perfectly
happy.

But after ten years of religious life, everything seemed
to be in ruins. Continually discouraged by changes of
Superiors, to whom she always became deeply attached,
she felt incapable of doing her job properly. Yet her job was
one of the easiest and was well below her potential. She
accused her Superiors of always sacrificing community life,
recreation, etc. to the demands of community work. In fact,
apart from an occasional charitable exchange, she had no
contact whatsoever with the other nuns. Apart from the
Superiors, she lived quite alone. Her emotional breakdown
(weeping, insomnia, and sexual temptations) seems to have
begun during a retreat, from which she remembers the
preacher's cold, implacable logic.

All her references to God are in terms of his kindness
and generosity: He will provide for her and protect her; the
perfect father will look after his unworthy child.

ATTITUDE TO BE ADOPTED BY THE COUNSELOR

We suggest the following procedure: a complete acceptance of the emotionally loaded remarks, encouragement of the fullest possible description of her miserable condition (tears), avoidance of the spiritual-emotional type of consolation. Also, it is wise to stick to the same theme: the religious community is not a family in the emotional sense of the word—true. The vow of chastity means that you always live alone—true. You are unworthy and, because of your character, you may be incapable of ever becoming a good nun—true. It is not good to attempt to channel the flow or restore awareness of reality, and her impassioned compensatory declarations about God's goodness should be ignored; they are unimportant and, in her present condition, they reveal in her declarations of faith an underlying psychological pattern which can scarcely be described as mature.

Obviously, we must be prepared for a considerable degree of transference, a violently emotional "shipwrecked-sailor" type of reaction (with a quiet prayer that the plank grabbed may not turn out to be an ordinary piece of driftwood). Also there must be a firm decision not to accept any changes in the schedule of fortnightly visits, which must never exceed the regular fifty minutes. Letters are to remain unanswered, and there are to be no telephone calls. The relationship should be maintained within these rigorously enforced limits: spiritual direction with emphasis on the psychological aspects.

If there is no noticeable improvement (superficial, at least) within three months, or if her suicidal tendencies reappear, the nun should be referred to a specialist.

CRITICAL PERIOD

No critical phase. The nun's fundamentally supernatural attitude produces continual psychoreligious syntheses as her psychic maturation progresses.

RESULT (AFTER TWENTY MONTHS)

Insomnia persists, but her appetite is back. Without resentment and thanks to our transference, she has had the courage to face up to and acknowledge the real difficulties of a religious life in itself, not only because of supposedly difficult circumstances but also, without despair, to acknowledge (not merely on the verbal level) her own relative unworthiness. She now accepts the fact that the community cannot be one big happy family. She is also beginning to realize that her own family upbringing was not as ideal as she had insisted at the beginning. With the help of a well-meaning onlooker, a less egocentric image of God is beginning to emerge from within herself.

Since I am (temporarily and at fixed hours) at her service, God no longer has to be. Together we can search for what is necessary for the greater glory of God. Christ is now the Saviour of mankind and no longer her psychic comforter. God's good faith consists in fulfilling his promises, but we cannot impose our own schedule. The Virgin Mary, excellent mother that she was, is seen as coredemptrix. Which is what the nun must now become, abandoning forever the good little girl of the past. Her signs of obedience are no longer the expression of a childish wish to be "good" but a symbolic surrender to God through the outward sign of submission to her lawful superiors.

ONE DIFFICULTY

By using the phenomenon of transference, a religious maturation has been psychologically achieved. But will I be able to sever the relationship or gradually reduce it without ruining everything?

I think so, for two reasons: first, another change of Superior has brought someone to the head of the community in whom the nun has complete confidence and to whom she is gradually opening out on an emotional level. Then she has decided to apply for a different assignment—perhaps for a year's study—which should mean that she will be able to do work more suited to her real talents. We must hope that her Superiors do not misinterpret her efforts as a sign of ambition and that they appreciate its true significance: an attempt on her part to free herself from crippling inhibitions and to put her adult personality to more effective use in the redemptive work which is always going on.

C. The growth of scrupulosity based on unconscious aggression

There is nothing of a "formula" about the following report, less so even than with the two preceding ones. The means of action proposed seem highly debatable when briefly outlined in this way. In our opinion, the final result might easily be described as a "stroke of luck." Yet we have included it both for the vigorous description and the clearness of the affective outburst.[14]

THE BEGINNING OF THE RELATIONSHIP

A twenty-five-year-old woman comes to see me because she is suffering from scruples. She claims that she has followed the advice of five priests and that her confessor finally told her she ought never to go to confession again and that, moreover, she was incapable of committing a mortal sin.

She seems terribly disappointed when I reply that under these circumstances I fail to understand why she should be in search of yet another priest.

Then she wants to know how a priest can possibly claim that a person has become incapable of committing mortal sin.

I reply, saying that quite frankly it seems to me that 1) such a statement seems extremely foolhardy; 2) that she is at perfect liberty to refuse to accept the suggestion, thus recapturing her "capacity for sin"; and that 3) she is

attempting in a typically aggressive fashion to set my opinion against her confessors.

She begins to sob. Priests, she says, can never reach agreement on this subject.

So I ask her what there is to stop her from undertaking
a fresh moral apprenticeship, that is, learning to distinguish
good from evil, to distinguish the petty fault from the grave
sin. She sighs, complaining that I am trying to force her
back into the agonies from which she has just escaped.

I insist, perhaps unwisely, that there is no alternative
course if she wishes to be cured. She jumps to her feet, cuts
short the interview, and leaves me with the impression that
I was probably too harsh with her and that, under the circumstances, I am not the man she is looking for.

Six months later

Another visit. She wants to go to confession. I insist on
a preliminary talk. She agrees and comes out with it, point-
blank: "You are the only priest I have ever met who has
told me that I have the right to sin!" There follows a fairly
labored account of past and present sexual failings. I do not
interrupt. When she has finished, I ask her, "Is that all?"
"Yes," she replies, "but I simply can't go on living if I
commit these mortal sins all the time."

I suggest that she come back to see me, that we will find
out whether or not she can pass objective judgment on
herself and gradually avoid real sins.

I am convinced that if she does return, it will be thanks
to the fact that she was able to express a certain hostility
in a tolerant atmosphere in which the usual hackneyed
response to her problems was turned completely upside
down.

Subsequent visits

Her entire psychomoral history emerges in the course of
five or six sessions: an almost terrifying ignorance in sexual

matters; parental discord; conscience nonexistent because torn between maternal and paternal superegos;* repressed hostility to anything connected with authority; "pitiable" behavior used as a means for upbraiding the world and its inhabitants.

Therefore, her re-education revolved around the fullest possible instruction in the problems of reproduction, explanations of the source of her moral doubts (lack of consistency in paternal and maternal commands), and, above all, around the discovery of the elementary and too often unacknowledged distinction between the order of moral values and the order of spiritual values and supernatural realities. Undoubtedly, Charity requires the practice of certain moral virtues, but this can often stem from thoroughly profane motives and, reciprocally, a lively awareness of our own moral failings can help to develop or to revive the temper of our conscience.

But this "instructional" aspect of our interviews could scarcely have improved the situation without the "emotional" aspect. This counselee discovered that she could express a certain measure of hostility (quite justifiably after the early moral-training fiasco) without losing a priest's sympathy. At the same time, she realized that from a psychological point of view, her relationship with God remained unaffected; on the contrary, she had remained remarkably untouched, since all the interior compulsions she had experienced as a victim (of her superego) had never allowed her to draw near and really experience that true liberty which belongs to the "adopted children," the brothers and sisters of Jesus Christ.

If the views expressed in this chapter are correct, and if

---

* The *superego* is an interior affective structure developed during the first six or seven years of life and influenced by the persons responsible for issuing the first educational commands, producing an automatic control over behavior and guilt feelings. It is an unconscious process of the conscience, with which it is often confused.

the excerpts from the three reports outlined above are worth bearing in mind as "examples," there is no need to be dismayed or discouraged by a pastoral relationship which starts off as a transference.

It is true that in many cases the priest will bear witness to God as "a veiled symbol." But the correct use of the symbolic process, which plays such an important role in religious life, will make the counselee realize that, considering his affective structures, it is only by means of this symbolic veil that God can reveal himself in the fullness of his mystery. As the slave of affective determinisms, first attaching himself to men in general and then to this man, the man of God in particular, the counselee will be able to resolve his transference only by splitting it in two: Dependent on an emotional level upon another man, the direction of his liberty and of his impulses (purified and spiritualized by the symbolic process) will be shifted and directed toward God, in whose salvatory action he believes without being affectively conscious of it or experientially aware of it.

As Madame Françoise Dolto so profoundly puts it: "Complete self-knowledge as a human being must involve an awareness that one is dependent upon sensory conditions, yet free within symbolic relationships."[15]

Thus, in order for a course of spiritual direction to be religiously fulfilled, some people will inevitably have to project their as yet unconscious and uncontrollable affective urges onto another man, gradually unfolding their spiritual purpose by an understanding of their symbolic significance.

In other words, many psychically immature counselees may have to discover the true meaning of priestly or even ecclesial mediation within the transference relationship itself. This is certainly one of the highest aims of genuine psychopastoral work.

From the preceding analyses and observations, the priest will note that as a religious and supernatural mediator, he will always be approached for reasons which lie outside or beyond himself.

Sometimes it will be because of the recognition and wholehearted acceptance of the symbolic and actual authenticity of his priestly behavior and pastoral care. In this case he will act as a priest: "He must become more and more, I must become less and less" (John 3:30).

Sometimes he will be approached as a mediator, but there will be some slight distortions in the actual concept of his role: here he will attempt to operate both as a priest and as a psychologist. Lucidly accepting these distortions as they come, he will use them as a major, if not the main, theme of his dialogue and of the proposed recovery: "If thou knewest what it is God gives . . . it would have been for thee to ask him instead" (John 4:10).

Lastly, he will certainly sometimes be faced with the barrier of a transference which he is not qualified to resolve nor even directly reveal; instead, he will have to bear with it without being duped by it, in order to divert its symbolically valid components toward divine charity, in a spirit of faith. These neurotic projections are the remnants of indeterminable primordial relationships, marring both the divine and the sacerdotal images. On such occasions, we should turn our thoughts to the mystery of Christ's death on the cross: "They will look upon the man whom they have pierced" (John 19:37). All human aggression exhausts itself on these heights of divine charity which pardons all things while remaining pure love, and, in doing so, reopens the paths of love. This is what will happen in the transference relationship if the priest, a religious mediator, also manages to fulfill the role of psychological mediator, using the transference obstacle, from which he himself suffers, to reveal its own hidden, supernatural significance.

Although the "pastoral resolution" of transference involves its separation into several affective component parts, only one part (that is, dependence or loving surrender) is destined to evolve on a spiritual level and to be directed authentically toward God by means of analogy and symbol. The remaining part (that is, aggression or insecurity) will be directed against the priest for perhaps a long time to come, quite literally crucifying him.

In the course of this "progress" of the pastoral relationship, the priest will have many opportunities for self-denial, especially when presented with the opportunity of taking part in a facile dialogue in which the more he is influenced by transference, the more misleading any insight gained will be.

He will also find ample food for his sense of humility. At the appropriate moment, he should repeat La Fontaine's remarks to the relic-carrying donkey:

> "Get these crazy, vain notions
> Out of your mind.
> It is the idol they are honoring
> And not you."

As for the counselees, if they belong to any of the groups described in the last half of this chapter, they should consider themselves fortunate to have experienced a transference relationship, and, more fortunate still, to have successfully outgrown it.

CHAPTER IV

A Method of Improving Group Supervision

IN THE COURSE OF the last fifty years, the psychology of human relations (observation, analysis of latent dynamisms, and systematic applications) has made rapid progress. Efforts are constantly being made by those responsible for the apostolic training of the clergy to apply the benefits of this progress, while at the same time guarding its own traditional, inspirational goals.[1]

The integration of psychological data and practices into the training of the clergy involves two distinct periods: before and after the beginning of the pastoral ministry; and two approaches—formative and informative.

1. *On the seminary level,* this will be a question of selecting and presenting the necessary psychological information to prepare a finely tuned awareness of the needs and attitudes of future counselees while at the same time protecting the student's own personal equilibrium. Some courses have already been introduced, and research has

been begun, sometimes accompanied by technical evaluation, into the content, the presentation, and the actual
effect of such courses.[2] Perhaps too great an emphasis is
placed, especially (for historical reasons) in the United
States,[3] on information concerning mental hygiene, relations with psychiatrists, and the prevention of mental
illness. But we should not ignore the fact that Protestant
pastoral work has benefited tremendously from participation in training programs in psychiatric and other types
of hospitals, where seminarists and young pastors practice
pastoral dialogue with the patients, under the careful supervision (based on their reports) of either a devoted psychologist or psychiatrist or of the chaplain in charge who,
in the United States at least, is usually a qualified psychologist.

Instead of attempting an examination of this line of
progress, we will refer the reader to certain specialized
publications.[4]

2. *When pastoral work has already begun,* opportunities must be sought and effective techniques devised for
ensuring additional psychological training. There is a need
to make good use of intensive workshops, specialized sessions, weekly work-study groups, and individual supervision.
These can be the occasions of conferences and discussion
groups, supervision of written or recorded reports, the acting of roles, psychodramas, etc. They will also take into
account the actual situation of "fully employed" members
of the clergy and the discretion which is essential in the
handling of pastoral dialogue.*

Naturally, we have no wish to exclude all theoretical
psychological knowledge from the work to be done with

---

* Care should be taken to make the pastor's relationship with a case
and not the case itself the focal point of all pastoral improvement methods;
this will help to avoid the risk of indiscretions which have sometimes proved
an unfortunate stumbling block in the widespread practice of "case work"
in social service.

priests already busy in parishes or schools. But we are convinced that in the majority of cases, all theoretical instruction should be subordinated to a greater psychological awareness of their own experience, their own attitudes, and of the very words they hear or utter in the course of pastoral dialogue.

In the course of so-called specialized training sessions, especially short-term ones limited to two or three days, it has become obvious that while descriptive or interpretative lectures may be invaluable and extremely helpful to specialists or priests with some psychological background, they can also present serious drawbacks: they frequently give rise to misunderstandings, to aggressively phrased objections, and even to misguided applications which are beyond control.

An intensive training session, lasting for at least five or six days, may certainly include one or two lectures each day. These should not last any longer than fifty minutes and should be followed by a question period. The most important part of the work is accomplished in small groups of ten to twelve people led by a specialist—a psychiatrist or psychologist—who should be aided by an observer. These groups meet twice a day for two hours at a time, and as far as possible they are left completely free to discuss their own interests and preoccupations. At first, the members of these groups will probably tend to raise theoretical problems. But thanks to their common calling and the sharing of similar interests, they will soon begin to raise psychological problems, probably in the form of case histories. This will gradually lead them to question their own case relations, i.e., the psychological attitudes which they adopt in pastoral work.*

* In fact, if this evolution is allowed to develop freely, a final stage will be reached in which some members of the group will begin to raise strictly personal problems, putting their very personality in question. Normally these sessions are too short to reach that stage. But, as will be shown

Once again, the reader who wishes to learn about the systematic experiments and research used to improve the program in these intensive sessions is referred to the appropriate publications.[5]

We are going to describe in much greater detail the work of another group-improvement experiment: weekly working groups of twelve to fifteen priests registered for fifteen to twenty meetings. We have observed these groups in action for the last nine years.*

Supervision Groups

The average member, priest or religious, of one of these groups finished his theology courses with an impressive array of clearly perceived ideas, excellent principles, and the very best intentions, all of which he has since tended to dispense in his pastoral dialogue without always having a very clear notion of his counselee's real attitudes. Naturally enough, this has led to failures, disillusionment, and disappointments, which are soon corrected by practical formulas for avoiding them or at least reducing their effect, and which are heightened by trying to understand the counselee in terms of some psychological technique (such as the study of personality) or by reading a psychology book (often a discussion of psychoanalytic theory from the religious point of view).

If initial good intentions gave rise to hasty words, recourse to these ready formulas will very often lead instead

---

later, the group leader would do well to avoid this approach, characteristic of group therapy. In our opinion, group supervision evolves more successfully if it concentrates on case relations.

* On the initiative of the *École des Parents et des Éducateurs*, 99, rue Belliard, Brussels 4, Belgium. A seminar of this type is offered every year to priests studying at the International Institute *Lumen Vitae*, 184, rue Washington, Brussels 5, Belgium.

to clichés or even to egocentric attitudes which are obviously much more difficult to correct. With these three types of psychologically defective pastoral dialogue in mind, we will now describe the activities, the development, and the problems of these supervision groups.

1 *Hasty words: a reduced awareness of the counselee*

The new curate, Father Z, called on a childless couple in which both husband and wife earn large salaries and thus live a relatively easy life. They spoke of their increasing estrangement, both in regard to sex and their leisure-time activities, and of a growing irritation with many details of their married life. Father Z pointed out the seriousness of the situation, saying it would get worse unless they took energetic steps to make it better. "Life together implies renunciation," he told them, adding that the sacrament uniting them called for self-denial, faithfulness, and generosity. If only they would be willing to forgo some of their material comforts and have a baby, the grace of God would not be denied them and they would know the joys of a true Christian marriage.

At the dinner table that night, Father Z told his Superior and the other curates about the difficulties he had encountered in his house-to-house visiting. He repeated the words his pastoral zeal had inspired. His colleagues were deeply impressed by this display of supernatural fervor, and by his unselfishness and courage in proclaiming the word of God.

At another meal, six months later, someone asked Father Z, in passing, about the problem family he had mentioned so discreetly and toward which he had adopted such a positive line of approach. How were things going? Not at all well, it seemed. Both parties were in touch with their lawyers, and divorce proceedings were under way.

So had it, in fact, been advisable to praise the pastoral zeal and the supernatural fervor of Father Z? Would it not have been better to query the advisability of his declarations, however moving they may have seemed to his perhaps less courageous colleagues? Would it not have been better if he had attempted to see things from the point of view of the couple to whom he was speaking, and to seek a fuller awareness of their actual dispositions and their real problems, thus making sure that they would listen to him when he spoke?

This communal examination of the opportuneness of remarks made is probably one of the most immediate advantages of supervised groups. A certain amount of discretion is required; the anonymity of the persons described must be respected. For this reason, it is best for the group to consist of priests who do not know each other or who do not, at least, usually work together. But a certain amount of confidence is also necessary: each person should be prepared to give an account of an interview or a part of one, reproducing as far as possible the actual words used at the most important and the most critical moments of a dialogue.[6]

The other members of the group will say what they felt when listening to the report and will then give their reactions to the counselor's replies, making a special effort of the imagination to see things from the perspective of the counselee.

We also make a point of rapidly asking the opinion of every member of the group concerning a given situation (e.g., interrupting the reading of a report at a characteristic or particularly ambiguous moment). Each person is asked to make an imaginative effort and say what the counselee might have felt at that moment or, alternatively, what he would have said in the counselor's place. In the light cast by this confluence of different perspectives,* any defects in the counselor-counselee relationship often stand very

* The term "perspective" is here used in its most literal sense: a partial vision of an object, resulting from a particular point of view.

sharply revealed. We also believe that it stimulates each member's imagination. In listening to other people's experiences, he discovers aspects of the problem which would not otherwise have occurred to him, and this creates the necessary conditions for a fuller awareness of another person's true condition.

2 *The use of clichés: a lack of flexibility*
   in counseling relationships
However useful theological studies and traditional religious training may be for learning the message to be preached and for developing the necessary moral and charitable dispositions, they have very little effect in themselves upon attitudes linked to the psychological personality of priests, the over-all style of their dialogue, and the type of relationship offered to their counselees.

Professor Jean Maisonneuve distinguishes* four main styles in contemporary counseling as practiced by doctors, lawyers, psychologists, social workers, etc.

In the authoritative style, more or less direct attempts are made to impose the counselor's point of view on the counselee, to suggest fresh courses of action, to evaluate or interpret the elements of the situation as described by the counselee and assume that he will accept this interpretation or evaluation. The attitudes inherent in this style, which may be either autocratic or paternalist, are usually expressed in the following types of reply: judicative, direct questioning, interpretative, or exhortatory.

In the manipulative style, attempts are made to influence other people, both against their will and without their knowledge, using skillful (supposedly) psychological maneuvers. The attitudes and expressions corresponding to this style are: outright encouragement, diplomatically pro-

* In "Techniques de psychologie sociale," *Bulletin de Psychologie* (Paris), March 1, 1959, pp. 621–627.

posed advice, good-willed suggestions, and help offered in
a roundabout manner.

In the elucidative style, the counselee is provided with an
opportunity for an increased awareness of his own problem,
for a greater intellectual grasp of its multiple aspects, and
for an improved perception (with greater clarity and security) of all its implications. Careful questioning and understanding are the characteristic attitudes of this style, which
deserves to be called "Socratic," or "maieutic."

In the co-operative style, the counselee is helped to seek
his own solution to the problem and helped to bear the
load of the emotional currents that are sweeping him along.
His own point of view and his own rhythm are constantly
accepted. A warm welcome is the mainspring of this type of
dialogue, which deserves the title "empathic."

A survey of current conversational reactions among five
hundred people (academics but not psychologists) shows
that the most frequent replies reveal interrogative, evaluative, or helpful attitudes. In other words, a great majority
of the replies fall into the authoritative or manipulative
categories.

TYPES OF REPLY

	Evaluative %	Interrogative %	Supporting %	Interpreting %	Understanding %
500 people	35	25	23	10	7
60 psychology students					
male	23	35	20	17	5
female	21	35	29	11	4

Among the sixty psychology students, the number of
evaluative replies is down in favor of interpretative and
interrogative replies—without in any way modifying the
over-all picture.

Although no statistics are available, our experience of
group work among priests leads us to believe that evalua-

tive replies (i.e., a very special modality of the "directive" function) seem to predominate among members of the clergy.

Within the group, an individual awareness of the different styles will produce a painstaking analysis of the words actually used by counselors, whether they come from a member's verbal report[7] or from printed versions of conversations (fictional or previously obtained), edited and distributed in advance as an analytical exercise for each member.

It is a question, therefore, of helping each person to become aware of his own spontaneous style, of the limitations of his "verbal keyboard," and to extend this in order to become capable of providing a greater variety of useful replies, no longer geared to the counselor's personal habits but to the needs of the counselee.

The method of role-playing can be immensely helpful, provided that the group leader introduces it without interrupting the progress of the group—that is, using it as a light dramatization of a conversation or story which has already been started in the course of conversation. Instead of using the third person ("Then this young man told me that . . ."), one slips into the first and second persons ("And so I answered, 'Tell me, why do you think that you . .?' "), suggesting that another member continues to express, in his own way, the replies of the young man in question. After a few minutes of this, the roles are reversed. This is an important moment for an awareness of certain obstacles which were holding up the dialogue, both for the two individuals playing the roles and for the members of the group who will later be discussing what they themselves would have said.

On more than one occasion we have seen someone who was virtually paralyzed when playing the counselor's role but who performed brilliantly when his turn came to play the counselee, piling up difficulties and expressing them

with such warmth and vivacity that there was scarcely a
shadow of doubt (even in his own eyes) of his personal
involvement in the difficulties described by the counselee.
The net result of all this work is an extension of the
verbal keyboard at the counselor's disposal, a greater flexibility in his replies and in his own personal style, a broader
range of potential relationships with different counselees
because of a greater adaptation to their own needs, and a
gradual abandonment of all cliché-ridden, egocentric attitudes. This applies, at least when the counselor's personality is not too deeply marked by an effectively structured
psychic egocentricity which may very well exist alongside
immense moral generosity. An awareness of this will be
much harder to attain, but it will be greatly facilitated by
one final aspect of group supervision.

3   *Egocentric remarks: a psychic defect in the counselor*
Sometimes, as a result of the complex relationships involved between individual members, between individuals
and the leader, or between the entire group and the leader,
group activity may provoke a stereotyped reaction in which
certain members express to the group or to the leader attitudes and reactions similar to those prevailing in their own
pastoral activity. This situation becomes invaluable when
it is technically well exploited in order to provoke that vivid
awareness and emotionally charged insight which is necessary if this adverse and often unconscious attitude is to be
successfully re-formed.

This type of situation requires extremely careful handling and, in our opinion, it should remain infrequent in
group supervision. In itself, the explication of this genuine
transference belongs in group therapy. The very personality
of a member is called into question (not only his counselee
relations), and there is a risk that the group will be side-
tracked, even if only for a short time, from its common
task, and concentrate its entire attention on one member,
which may make him extremely nervous.

Ideally, the person himself, helped perhaps by one or two subtle or even mischievous hints from the rest of the group, should suddenly be surprised by something which he has always taken for granted elsewhere. An example follows:

Father W is taking part in the fifteenth meeting of a group in which he has played an extremely active role. During the discussion of his report of a pastoral interview, several of the other members were struck not only by the acuity of his intellectual welcome but also by his tendency to disregard the emotional aspects of the counselee's remarks. His inclination was to reassure the counselee, encourage him, generalize certain aspects of the problem as described, and play down his more vigorous expressions with a touch of humor. This would have been charming if it had not been overdone. In short, the slightest hint of anxiety in the dialogue was immediately neutralized by Father W.

During the discussion of his report, Father W was quite willing to admit all this, but on a purely intellectual plane. "Yes, I see," he said, "but . . ." He also provided himself with an alibi by claiming that in fact he had not been quite so reassuring as his written report might lead one to believe. Then he justified himself by saying he believed that the counselee had been in real need of reassurance. Obviously, he was the only person who could be the final judge of this.

Here is a transcript of part of the discussion during the fifteenth session. Father Y has just finished reading his report:

FATHER Y: I'd like to know what all of you think. I don't think I succeeded with this young lady.

FATHER W: *All the same, you did comfort her.*

FATHER Y: I don't have that impression. When she left, she seemed more bewildered than ever.

FATHER W: *That often happens. All the same, she did say, "I feel much better after telling you all this."*

FATHER Y: Oh, she was just being polite.

FIRST MEMBER: I'd like to know why Father W is trying to reassure Father Y.

SECOND MEMBER: Yes. Why not accept what Father Y says when he tells us, "I don't think I succeeded"?

FATHER W: *I'm willing to accept anything you like. It's just that I believe Father Y did better that he thinks.*

FIRST MEMBER: Would it really bother you to have to admit that Father Y had failed in this case?

FATHER W: *Ah! I see. You asked the same question when we were discussing the person mentioned in my report. So you think I'm always trying to reassure people . . .*

FATHER Y: Personally, I would rather hear all of you agree that I failed with this counselee. Then perhaps you will help me to find out why . . . (Silence.)

A little later, during the same session:

FATHER Y: *We all seem very touchy today.* (Laughter.)

THIRD MEMBER: We've often strayed away from the main topic today. As if we are all worried or dissatisfied with the results achieved during the group meetings.

FATHER W: *It's probably the same with all groups when they near their end.*

FIRST MEMBER: There's Father W, trying to reassure us again.

LEADER: And show us that we are quite a good group after all.

SECOND MEMBER: Father W, whom exactly are you trying to reassure?

FATHER W (half-joking, half-serious): *Well, now you've got me. It's perfectly true, though. On my way here today, I said to myself that the life of a group like this is certainly very short, and at the point we've reached, none of us will gain very much from it. . . . Now I see the true reason behind my remarks. But is it possible that I behave in the same way with my counselees?*

As can be seen by rereading his italicized remarks, Father W moves rapidly toward an awareness which is no longer purely intellectual but also emotional, the only kind capable of leaving its mark and of transforming or affecting—be it ever so slightly—his future attitude.

Father W was able to spot his tendency to react always in the same way and was led to suspect his self-centered motives, thanks to the two occasions within the group when he actually experienced his tendency to reassure and to play down any difficult situation (first concerning Father Y and later concerning possible deficiencies within the group itself). He was thus led to make the necessary deductions about his own pastoral reactions as they emerged from his report.

Lines of development

As we have seen, these supervision groups based on oral or written reports allow many different methods of training and improvement, such as role-playing and the discussion of transference relationships that emerge within the group. In our opinion, the latter task should rarely be undertaken.

The fact that many groups have to pass through the same stages as the specialized groups already mentioned does not, in our opinion, constitute an obstacle. These are: a) a stage in which theoretical discussion predominates; b) a stage in which a more or less objective discussion of different "cases" predominates; c) a stage in which discussions begin concerning counselee relationships and attitudes adopted during dialogue. Although the group leaders should look for methods to speed the group toward the final stage, they should realize that this process is more or less inevitable whenever intellectual adults get together to improve their knowledge of psychology.

Initial insecurity is gradually reduced in an atmosphere of free acceptance which is cautiously tested during the opening theoretical exchanges. As for the case-history phase, this can go on for a long time if the group leader shows too great an interest or seems to the other members of the group (even if they are mistaken) to consider it an ideal method of pastoral improvement. In the perspective which we suggest, the group leader is advised to concentrate explicitly on the actual words used, thus drawing attention to the attitudes adopted and the relationships established. Obviously, hundreds of cases can be discussed without the slightest change of attitude resulting. On the other hand, a priest who has succeeded in perfecting one attitude will be better equipped to deal with the thousand and one cases he will come across in the course of his own pastoral labors.

Here we must mention three psychological tendencies which seem sometimes to emerge as a result of the improvement itself.

a) Too sharp a reaction against the tendency to pass judgment or to evaluate the contents of a dialogue as expressed by the counselee can sometimes lead to a laissez-faire, or passive, attitude which takes the place of true welcome. By means of a highly technical and often artificial effort, a pastor striving to achieve the attitude recommended by the psychologists will merely reduce the power of his own presence by excessive censorship of his statements. In the best cases, this may be nothing but a temporary, compensatory reaction against excesses in the opposite direction. Still, it is well to mention it here in order to avoid the adoption by certain counselors of a cold, impassive air of detachment which is the very antithesis of the warm, personal welcome required for the establishment of a sound psychological and pastoral relationship. The fundamental requirements for any dialogue are presence and authenticity, and all true progress must stem from them.

b) A tendency toward an objectivist psychologism can result in a suspension of the process of getting to know our neighbor in the uniqueness of his development and of his conflicts. Quite apart from the hopeful promises of personality study, many priests expect psychologists to provide them with information on which they can make broad generalizations (as if we are talking about character types) such as: "Explain the attitude of women toward priests." "Describe for us the scrupulous mentality." "What are the psychological causes of masturbation?" etc. True, these are wonderful subjects for a psychologist-lecturer who wants to enthrall his audience with his view on "women," "scrupulosity," and "masturbation." But the clinical picture presented in such general terms will succeed only in mystifying any priests anxious to improve themselves and in search of practical techniques for use in their pastoral relations.

In a similar deep-seated and illusory search for an easy way out, many people are compelled to describe and discuss their "cases," i.e., objective situations, as if the neat solution of "one" case could be applied to all other "cases" in the same category. In groups seeking a complementary, formative effect, it is advisable to avoid a plethora of information which will only distract attention from a concern for the individual and will not improve that "unique colloquy" which is the essential moment in pastoral relations.

c) Finally, the members and leaders of the supervision groups, all of whom quite justifiably esteem *the mediative function* so highly, can begin to seek it *apart from the other two functions of welcome and guidance.* Toward the end of a well-handled interview in which his religious mediation has often been explicitly and implicitly at work, a priest may feel the need to provide some additional exhortation in terms having no direct reference to the words used by the counselee: "Our Lord also suffered," "You are sharing the humble life of the Virgin Mary," "Your sister is Martha and you are Mary. There is no need to feel ashamed." In general, religious symbols which are superimposed and incorrectly articulated to the counselee's needs and circumstances are listened to but rarely heeded. True, many priests act in this way without any psychological training, but we have observed that some priests, after making a special effort to improve their relations on a human level, often tend to accentuate this unfortunate dichotomy between psychological and religious activity. They seem to forget that their role and the image the counselee has of it is already acting as an extremely effective liaison between the human aspects of the dialogue and their supernatural significance.

In fact, the welcome and guidance functions (in the pastoral sense of the terms already discussed in Chapter II) are not readily distinguishable from the mediative function. When correctly fulfilled, they themselves are implicitly mediative (i.e., they point toward God), provided that the priest or one of his colleagues also acts as a sacramental mediator. The pastoral goal is always kept in mind, even when the topic of conversation is apparently a moral or psychological question. And if the different symbols and historical personalities of our faith appear in the conversation, as is their due, their psychological significance will be based on the fact that they are brought into play at the crucial moment when the welcoming and guidance functions are at work.

The goals of these supervision groups may therefore be defined as follows: to develop a capacity for awareness of other people (empathy); to match the psychological needs of counselees by extending the range of replies available; to introduce the Christian message on the basis of a fuller sacerdotal relationship, thanks to a more open and disinterested attitude toward other people.

It is certainly a great help if the group leader is a psychologist with a full command of the correct attitudes and techniques for improving human relations. Although his theological vocabulary may be limited, he should be aware of pastoral reality as encountered by priests, and he should have some knowledge of the supernatural sources from which their inspiration is drawn.

But even without a psychologist, these work-study groups can, we believe, be formed in a friendly spirit of mutual aid, especially if the priest-leaders have been fortunate enough to participate in a supervision group led by a psychologist or if they have at least received some elementary instruction in discussion group procedure.[8] After all, one does not have to be an expert in psychology in order to get together with a few friends to pool common doubts, difficulties, and hesitancies, and exchange views on the most successful attitudes and reactions. Each person thus benefits from the experience of all the others.

This final chapter is intended for priests anxious to enjoy the benefits of this type of supervision based on a spirit of friendly co-operation. In it we have described the goals, methods, and the main psychological "processes" which normally govern the life of these groups devoted to the improvement of psychological awareness.

CONCLUSION

Psychological and Pastoral Dialogue

> It is never wrong for people to speak freely to each other.
>
> Pope John XXIII on Ecumenism

ACCORDING TO an old saying, the spiritual counselor should make himself heard as "the outward voice of an inner consciousness."

The image that many priests have of their role in pastoral counseling, of this "outward voice," makes them tend to speak as "experts" on religious and moral issues. Although placed in a position of authority, they do their best to avoid all display of authority by means of a great effort of good will: they listen carefully, evaluate what they hear, and offer hasty judgment or advice. This approach corresponds to the image of the priestly function that many of the counselees hold. However, there is no denying that this image is undergoing rapid modification under various influences which may vary greatly in different countries and in different social classes. A growing number of the faithful—among the most dedicated and the most highly cultured in a religious and humane sense—now wish the priest to provide them with assistance, clarification, and stimuli along the lines of their religious development, but they no longer ask him for imperative advice, ready-made solutions, or cliché-ridden guidance. Many of them are already familiar with this type of reply; they have a vague desire for contact with a man who, seeing things from God's point of view alone, will help them to follow in the same direction and to acquire a loving and charitable perspective on the struggles in which they are involved. Before the priest speaks, they want him to listen to them and admit their right to have problems, to express them, and to live with them, perhaps even for a long time, before they grow to maturity in the warmth of interior grace.

At a time when all the "human-relations" professionals are making a serious effort to determine their own role, that is, the exact nature of the image and the expectations they have to fulfill in their contacts with other people, it seemed to us that the first requirement for the development of pastoral dialogue—especially in spiritual direction—was a greater awareness of the basis and the specific functions of pastoral relations.

From a psychological point of view, the characteristics of pastoral relations are so highly complex that no adequate comparison can be made with any other type of human relationship. It cannot be equated with the teaching relationship, from which all emotional expression is generally excluded; or the commanding relationship, which is often more concerned with execution than with motivation; or the medical relationship, strongly inclined toward physiological action; or the psychotherapeutic relationship, preoccupied as it is with psychic transference; or the family or parental relationships, based on affection and on biological and economic reality; or the friendly relationship, which calls for a reciprocal mutual exchange, even when one of the friends is an "expert" and thus a good counselor for the other. None of these can be used to describe the grandeur and specificity of the pastoral relationship which combines, in the name of God, unconditional acceptance, unselfish testimony, and gradual self-effacement.

Undoubtedly, the pastoral relationship is one in which a human being should be able to find the deepest and most authentic expression of the fullness of his beliefs, his conflicts, and his aspirations.

One man, generally a priest, who has undergone extensive spiritual training in preparation for his work in the service of others and who is sufficiently detached from family, economic, and political considerations, applies himself with all the powers of attention at his command to listening to the different situations, questions, and hesitations which another human being, his counselee, puts to him as the representative of God.

Opposite him there is the counselee who may be young or old, man or woman, rich or poor, but who is often hounded by social pressures; he turns to his chosen confidant, hoping to hear—quite apart from sound advice and moral instruction—the words by which this man reveals himself as the symbol of God.

Representative and symbol of God. What can these terms mean, except that the dialogue moves directly, if only because of the intentions present, into the perspective of the ultimate meaning of existence? This provides the finest possible attitude for the counselee's human and supernatural development, since it is marked by the two attributes of a biblical God and the God of Christian Revelation: a respect for liberty ("God is patient") and a benevolent love ("God is love").

The spiritual counselor, in the service of a brotherly

dialogue—a brotherhood based on the gratuitous initiative of divine adoption—must therefore learn to become this "man of God who said almost nothing to me, this priest to whom I turned when in need of enlightenment, of whom I thought when I needed to rediscover in my own way the image of God." (G. Zilboorg)

Neither theology nor personal sanctity can provide adequate training for this task; a systematic effort must be made to develop the necessary attitudes and abilities required in dialogue.

People often complain about insufficient attention being given to spiritual direction, about a lack of interest in pastoral consultations, without which adult Christians cannot be properly formed. In fact, experience has shown that most priests devote an extremely limited amount of time to these personal interviews even when they could, if they wished—as is often the case—set aside at least one hour a week and, at the most, ten per cent of their working time. Few priests consider these "private conferences" as playing a vital role in their priestly tasks. Rare are those who continue them regularly over a period of time. Rarer still are the ones who systematically question themselves as to the exact goals of their work or the actual effectiveness of their actions, the words they use, and the relationships they form.

There is no need to be surprised, therefore, at the rarity of well-managed spiritual direction, at the tendency of counselees to turn to other counselors, while maintaining a strictly sacramental relationship with the priest; at the discouragement of so many people who are unable to find even one psychological counselor in the religious field. Reality will always have its revenge when its complexity remains unrecognized.

On the other hand, a re-evaluation is currently taking place under the twofold influence of a more mature grasp of the Christian message—for example, the many new works on catechetics—and of a growing interest in the psychological aspects of pastoral work. Today a closer investigation of the meaning of the Word of God is thus happily allied to progress in human dialogue: Greater care taken over the teaching of the Word is supported by a closer attention to men's spoken words, an indispensable condition for authentic dialogue.

Is the psychology of human relations ready to be of service in this work of perfection?

Certainly from a Christian point of view, this would be its greatest achievement. Also, as a priest and a psychologist, it remains the author's dearest wish—one which he has attempted to share with the reader of this book.

APPENDIX

The Research Viewpoint

The priest's role and parental images

THE MAIN BODY of this book is designed for actual working use. However, it now seems appropriate to introduce a theme for observation and study: the incidence (in theory and practice) of parental images in pastoral relations. This quest for the unknown will have a greater appeal for theologians or psychologists engaged in scientific research, but it will also, we hope, be of interest to anyone for whom pastoral theory is not merely a collection of ready-made, culturally acceptable formulas.

The growth of any branch of science always involves a new series of fundamental questions for which scientific discoveries themselves gradually provide at least partial answers, sometimes provoking a whole new series of even more basic questions.

Scientific progress in the psychology of human relations has been accompanied by a growing awareness of the importance of roles* and of the complexity of the images held of these roles

* Social psychology uses the "role" concept to describe a pattern of behavior stemming from an individual's position in a group and socially

in the very heart of the most familiar interactions: the marital relationship, for example, or the parental one. Thus the father's and the mother's roles are lived in a different manner in a matriarchal and in a patriarchal society and again in a collective culture such as that of an Israeli kibbutz or that expressed in Soviet pedagogy.

When applied to pastoral relations, the "role" concept becomes more complicated but also more worth while because of a symbolic or analogical connotation: a dialogue with a priest unfolds, so to speak, "on a divine background" and within the perspective of the ultimate meaning of existence, calling all human relations into question. To say that the priest appears as a "parent substitute" or that his role is based upon "an image of authority" might be an interesting observation from a genetic point of view, possibly helpful for explaining the attitudes brought to pastoral relations by certain counselees and the different shades of meaning in the subsequent dialogues. But these psychological interpretations certainly fail to reach the heart of the problem which, in our opinion, is first and foremost theological. They fail to provide an answer to the fundamental question: What is the psychological significance of the opening of a dialogue relationship with a priest whose duty it is to act as a "representative of God" and even, in Christianity, in the name and place of Jesus Christ, the Son of God, who became flesh in order to save mankind?

A series of questions are beginning to develop around this theme. They will gradually be asked in many more minds, thanks to recent developments in psychology as applied to pastoral work.

We have tried to draw up a short list of these questions, addressing the appropriate ones to theologians, and directing others concerning research and the study of facts to representatives of the applied sciences (the psychosociology of human relations and applied psychology). On this level, the latter type

structured by the expectations of other members of the group (the image which the other make of it).

of question will be answered only if research centers (especially institutes of psychology or sociology in Catholic universities) decide to guide the work of their personnel and their available techniques in this direction.

I Questions raised in a theological perspective

a) Since the priest's Christian mediation leads to salvation in Jesus Christ by "adoption," is it expedient (desirable? obligatory?) for it to take psychological form in a relationship marked by certain father-son type characteristics in the course of pastoral dialogue?

Even psychologically speaking, this must be considered as an analogy, since relations with the priest transcend all biological relationships.[1]

b) Assuming the answer to the first question to be in the affirmative, is it more consistent with theological thought for a relationship to be established with a priest in which the counselee (man *or* woman) will display certain characteristics appropriate to a paternal image? Or will the psychic characteristics of a maternal image also fit the specifications?[2]

c) Does the theologian, familiar with Christian sources in the Old and New Testaments and with the tradition and history of pastoral work, consider it expedient (desirable? obligatory?) that psychological characteristics other than those inspired by parental relationships should appear and remain in the pastoral dialogue: brotherly friendship, for example, or the master-pupil relationship, or again, a carefully maintained "distance" relationship (based on a reverential awe of a "sacred" personality, even in pastoral interviews)?

In order to study this question of an "archetypal" (i.e., a primordial, culturally dynamic) image of the priest in the Judaeo-Christian tradition *and* in a theological perspective (i.e., in theory and not only in observed fact), it will probably be necessary to subject the attributes of the priestly function (in the Jewish, Old Testament tradition) to a historical and critical examination, concentrating on the prophetic mission on the one hand and on the royal mission on the other.[3]

II   Questions raised in a sociocultural perspective

a) Are the historical connections between the priestly role and other similar roles such as those of the healer (protective magic) or the sorcerer (hostile magic) a constant factor in religious attitudes and behavior? Or are they just the expression of a primitive religiosity that gradually fades away and finally disappears altogether in the more "sophisticated" religions, in Buddhism, for example, and especially in the Judaeo-Christian tradition?

This problem is raised here as a question of fact. If raised in a Christian perspective "in theory," it would be the theologian's business.

b) Assuming an affirmative answer to the last part of the previous question, would it be possible to trace a psychological line of demarcation and discrimination between attachment to the "wizard" and attachment to the priest?

In other words, can this frequently made distinction actually be applied (i.e., verified, by means suitable for the psychology of the persons involved) according to which relationships with "magical" individuals (even modern "sorcerers" such as astrologers, fortunetellers, and healers) respond to the needs and functions of the "superego," while the relationship with the priest is functionally centered on the growth of the ego?[4] But, in fact, would we not often find exactly the opposite?

III   Questions raised in a psychological perspective

a) Has the relationship with God a greater psychological affinity with the father or with the mother image? Or with a combination of the two? Or perhaps with other images which, theologically speaking, seem less central: the leader of the people (king)? The military leader (adonai)? The good shepherd? The keeper of morality (the judge)? The physician ("medicus animae")? The bridegroom ("sponsus-sponsa")?[5]

b) Supposing that in living Christianity, the relationship with God has, in fact, a greater affinity with some of these images (even taking age, sex, and cultural and social differences into account), does this tend to increase or, on the contrary, to diminish among the elite, fervent Christians with a highly developed life of prayer, possibly even among mystics?[6]

c) Does the relationship with the priest have the same psychological affinities as the relationship with God? (See above.) Or are these affinities reversed, perhaps? As a guiding hypothesis, it will be remembered that the title "Father" is used when it is a question of "God the Father," but that "Mother" is usually used to describe "Our Mother, the Church." Psychologically speaking, in which of these two directions is the relationship with the priest actually lived?[7]

d) Assuming that a relationship with the priest displays one or other of the above affinities, would this not tend to gradually retard Christian growth toward human and spiritual maturity? It will be necessary here to take differences in age and social and family conditions into account.[8]

IV *Questions raised in a psychopastoral perspective*
   (actual application)

a) What are the most effective attitudes and techniques for developing a pastoral relationship that will be a psychological realization of its theological nature, bearing in mind the actual dispositions of the counselee at the beginning of his pastoral dialogue?

b) What are the most appropriate attitudes and techniques for restoring this psychologically and pastorally desirable relationship when it is poorly structured from the start (e.g., by transference or by specifically cultural connections: passive dependence, superstition, etc.)?

When, thanks to the combined efforts of theologians and psychologists, we are able to provide answers to these questions, we will be able to enjoy a fuller and surer awareness of the psychological position of the Church in the world and of the means by which the pastoral work of its priests can continue in human dialogue, thus providing a fuller, richer expression of the charity of the Word incarnate.

Notes and Bibliography

Introduction: The Current Position of Pastoral Psychology

1. Five major works are required reading for anyone wishing to learn about the current state of pastoral psychology in the United States. The first two are by Catholics:

Charles A. Curran. *Counseling in Catholic Life and Education* (Preface by Eugène Cardinal Tisserant). New York: Macmillan, 1952.

George Hagmaier, C.S.P., and Robert Gleason, S.J. *Counseling the Catholic: Modern Techniques and Emotional Conflicts.* New York: Sheed & Ward, 1959.

Seward Hiltner. *Pastoral Counseling.* New York: Abingdon, 1949.

Wayne E. Oates. *Protestant Pastoral Counseling.* Philadelphia: Westminster Press, 1962.

Carroll A. Wise. *Pastoral Counseling.* New York: Harper & Row, 1951.

There are at least two works in German which express the question well: E. Ringel and W. van Lun. *Die Tiefenpsychologie hilft dem Seelsorger.* Vienna: Herder, 1952; Adelheid Rensch. *Das seelsorgerliche Gespräch.* Göttingen: Vandenhoeck und Ruprecht, 1963.

Father R. Hostie's *Le Dialogue Pastoral* (Bruges: Desclée De

Brouwer, 1963) is the outstanding work in French. (An English translation is in preparation.)

A book by Henri Bissonnier, *Introduction à la psychopathologie pastorale* (Paris: Éditions Fleurus, 1960) is mainly theoretical, but its over-all perspective is good.

Several volumes of *Études Carmélitaines* (Bruges: Desclée De Brouwer) are of value in this context, especially the following volumes: *Direction Spirituelle et Psychologie* (1951); *Trouble et Lumière* (1949), English Edition—*Conflict and Light* (Sheed & Ward); *Technique et Contemplation* (1949); *Mystique et Continence* (1952); *Limites de l'Humain* (1953).

There is a classic pastoral psychology manual, preceding recent developments, which emphasize the importance of the "relational" aspect: Willibald Demal, O.S.B., *Praktische Pastoralpsychologie*, 2nd ed., Wien: Herder, 1953. This systematic survey describes especially the counselee mentality, examining it according to age, sex, type and temperament, social class, pathological divisions, etc. Several translations have been made, including *Pastoral Psychology in Practice*, New York: P. J. Kenedy, 1955.

Several magazines study the psychological aspect of pastoral problems and should be consulted:

Journal of Pastoral Care (Council for Clinical Training, 475 Riverside Drive, New York, N.Y.) A Protestant publication.

Pastoral Psychology (Pastoral Psychology Press, Manhasset, New York). A Protestant magazine, whose pastoral consultant is Seward Hiltner. In February, 1959, it published a special issue edited entirely by Catholics: "Catholic Viewpoints in Pastoral Psychology."

Catholic Counselor (Iona College, New Rochelle, N.Y.)

Insight (3140 Meramec St., St. Louis 18, Mo.) A quarterly review of religion and mental health, whose editor is Father Fintan McNamee, O.F.M.

In addition to works in English, the reader with a knowledge of French might wish to consult the following:

Christus (35, rue de Sèvres, Paris VI). A special issue on spiritual direction (January, 1960, No. 25) and some articles (not enough) on the psychological aspects of spiritual discernment.

Études (15, rue Monsieur, Paris VII). Frequent contributions by Father Louis Beirnaert, S.J.

Notes de Pastorale familiale (supplement to *Feuilles Familiales*, 54 rue Marie de Bourgogne, Brussels 4). Psychological problems of the family, love, and sexuality are often well discussed in connection with priestly work.

Présences (Prieuré Saint-Jean, Champrosay-Draveil, France), especially the issues *Santé, maladie et vie spirituelle* (Vol. II, 1955); *Le malade mental* (Vol. I, 1956); *Le malade mental et son entourage* (Vol. I, 1960); *La foi et les malades* (Vol. II, 1961).

Psyché. The 120 numbers of the collection, published between 1946 and 1957, form a set in which the pastoral psychologist will find interesting conferences on many "objective" topics (anxiety, guilt, case histories, etc.) but not on the pastoral relationship as such.

Supplément de la Vie Spirituelle (29, Boulevard Latour-Maubourg, Paris VII). The most important collection of theoretical, descriptive, and bibliographical studies on relationships in the spiritual life and the factors which affect them. Good decennial index in a special booklet (1947–1957).

In addition, the *Dictionnaire de Spiritualité* is now being published (Paris, Beauchesne). Much space is devoted to often excellent articles on psychological theory, providing a clear indication of the contemporary approach. In particular, we would like to mention "Anormaux" by J. de Tonquédec; "Ascèse" and "Chasteté" by A. Willwoll; "Conscience" by R. Carpentier; "Crises Affectives" by J. MacAvoy; "Culpabilité" by C. Baudouin and L. Beirnaert; "Direction spirituelle et Psychologie" by J. MacAvoy; "Enfant (vie spirituelle)" by P. Ranwez; "Expérience" by A. Léonard; "Extase" by H. Gratton.

Although not concerned primarily with pastoral counseling, the symposium *Cross Currents of Psychiatry and Catholic Morality* (New York, Pantheon Books, 1964) is worth consulting because it provides translations of key articles by many of the major French contributors to the current dialogue between religion and psychiatry: Louis Beirnaert, S.J., Albert Plé, O.P., Jacques Maritain, Jean Rimaud, S.J., Bruno de Jésus Marie, O.C.D., Maryse Choisy, and others.

The following German publication should also be noted: *Anima* (Seelsorgeinstitut der Universität Freiburg, Switzerland), edited by Dr. Franz X. von Hornstein.

2. The use of typology in the study of personality (Kretschmer or Spranger in Germany, Heymans or Le Senne in France, and Sheldon in the United States) will certainly provide the young pastoral psychology student with his first taste of human diversity in a certain way of looking at the realities of the world and its inhabitants, and of adapting and reacting to them. One of our pupils published a study of spiritual direction from this point of view: Henri Simoneaux, O.M.I., *Spiritual Guidance and the Varieties of Character*, New York, Pageant Press, 1956. His conclusions are reviewed and commented upon in "Direction Spirituelle et Caractère," *Nouvelle Revue Théologique* (Louvain), March, 1956, pp. 271–291. In practice, however, this personality study approach is seen to be deceptive; it is not worth the time the counselor spends learning it. The brief remarks on this subject in our Introduction should not be interpreted as a complete rejection of the study of individual traits (no more than of the different categories which serve as indications in psychopathology. See the author's *Guide pour discerner les troubles mentaux*, 2nd ed., Brussels: Editions de l'Oeuvre des Tracts, 1962). These descriptions are, we believe, useful insofar as they lead to further study and an increased awareness of the different kinds of relationships that can exist between the counselor and the different "types" (normal or pathological) under consideration.

3. Many educators (and pastoral counselors are no exception) turn to psychology in the hope of finding formulas, practical systems, means of influencing other people "in the right way," and easy methods for obtaining success at low cost. This is very human, perfectly understandable, and even excusable. Also the urge to dominate exists in the most refined human relationships, and psychologists are not miraculously immune to it any more than spiritual directors.

Their partnership begins to deteriorate when the psychologist consciously enters into the act, offering spiritual counselors the false advantage of ready-made techniques whose aim will turn out to be nothing more than a sort of conditioning process or psycho-pastoral seduction. Some popularized psychology publications designed for the use of the American clergy do not escape this temptation to facility. For example: O. A. Battista, author of *The*

Power to Influence People, Englewood Cliffs, N. J., Prentice-Hall, 1959, cites the testimony of a clergyman friend to prove the worth of his section on the religious field, "Ten methods of influencing people." The same tendency to provide ready-made formulas sometimes spoils Paul F. Douglass's *The Group Workshop Way in the Church* (New York, Association Press, 1956) which contains some useful chapters on the life of groups within a parish framework. It is well known that books on how to command, how to find a wife, and how to improve your memory are of little use except to those already generously endowed with the necessary qualities. And of course it has been ironically suggested that "how to get rich" worked only for the author and his publisher.

Yet it would not be so bad if the priest-victims of such fake promises were simply disappointed. Unfortunately, some of them go much further, declaring that if that is all psychology has to offer them, then . . . In fact, what true psychology will slowly begin to offer pastoral counselors will be a gradual re-examination of themselves in their relationships with their counselees. Not a ready-made formula for making the work easier but a signpost to bring it closer to reality. This, it must be admitted, is often much more difficult.

Besides, there is always a temptation to transform any means of making pastoral-psychological attitudes more flexible into a mechanical process. Chapters I and II of this book are not immune to this danger, especially the analyses of the "reflective" and "elucidative" techniques. However, by constantly calling the personality of the counselor himself into question, we hope to have forewarned the reader against the possible false illusion of claiming to be able to help other people without first opening himself to them.

Moreover, if theoretical and technical instruction is of little use in the psychology of human relations, we believe that contact with the masters in this field (especially the great representatives of clinical psychology), listening to their recorded interviews, analyzing their replies, and reading accounts of conferences they have supervised will be immensely valuable in improving psychopastoral training—a value which can be assured only by submitting one's own work to one of them, occasionally at least, or in a group.

4. Some books of great humane and technical value for improving psychological relations in secular subjects sometimes encounter reservations from the clergy because the books do not deal with their current preoccupations, and are written in an unfamiliar style. It must be admitted that the reading of such works involves a constant effort to adapt them to a pastoral perspective. Still, in the absence of a more abundant literature on pastoral psychology, these books can still be extremely useful, especially as further reading for counselors who have already clarified their own pastoral goals. We would recommend the following books in this category:

Félix Biestek, S.J. *The Casework Relationship*. Chicago: Loyola University Press, 1957.

Charles Nahoum. *L'entretien psychologique*. Paris: Presses Universitaires de France, 1958.

Carl Rogers and G. Marian Kinget. *Psychothérapie et relations humaines*. 2 volumes, Paris and Louvain, Nauwelaerts, 1962.

Social Casework in Marital Problems (A study by a group of caseworkers). London: Tavistock Publications, 1955.

5. The scientific study of the laws governing the establishment and development of relationships between counselors and counselees has never been taken so far as in the psychotherapeutic school of Carl Rogers in Chicago. On this subject, the following books should be mentioned:

Rogers, Carl R. *Client-Centered Therapy*. Boston: Houghton Mifflin, 1959.

———. *Counseling and Psychotherapy*. Boston: Houghton Mifflin, 1942.

———. *On Becoming a Person*. Boston: Houghton Mifflin, 1961.

———, and Dymond, Rosalind F. *Psychotherapy and Personality Change*. Chicago: University of Chicago Press, 1954.

Snyder, William. *The Personality Relationship*. New York: Macmillan, 1961.

As yet, no means seems available for undertaking such detailed research in the field of pastoral relations. Goals in this area are so complex (see Chapter II) and have such a strictly religious aspect that they are often not subject to empirical observation or control. It is even necessary to raise the question as to whether it will ever be possible to consider them, even from their human aspect, using strict scientific methods.

On the other hand, one cannot help feeling disturbed by the growing gap between the care taken by different groups of social workers (welfare workers, for example, using the case work method, often involve themselves in long, expensive supervisions) to improve themselves long *after* the completion of their training, and the empiricism which is still the rule in ecclesiastical circles. The embarrassment of a young priest in a delicate pastoral situation is generally "resolved" by recourse to a friend, to an experienced priest, or to a professor in the seminary. Thus the stage of "catch-all" solutions is soon reached, in which routine often replaces fully thought-out experience.

6. Religious counselors might find the following list of books valuable:

Bingham, W., Moore, B., and Gustad, J. *How to Interview*, 4th ed. New York: Harper & Row, 1959.

Blum, M., and Balinsky, B. *Counseling and Psychotherapy*. Englewood Cliffs, N. J.: Prentice-Hall, 1951.

Bordin, E. *Psychological Counseling*. New York: Appleton, 1955.

Brayfield, A. *Readings in Modern Methods of Counseling*. New York: Appleton, 1950.

Buchheimer, A., and Barlogh, Sara. *The Counseling Relationship*. Chicago: Science Research, 1961.

Cottle, W. C., and Downie, N. M. *Procedures and Preparation for Counseling*. Englewood Cliffs, N. J.: Prentice-Hall, 1960.

Kahn, L., and Cannell, C. *The Dynamics of Interviewing*. New York: Wiley, 1957.

Loughary, J. W. *Counseling in Secondary Schools*. New York: Harper & Row, 1961.

McGowan, J. F., and Schmidt, L. D. *Counseling: Readings in Theory and Practice*. New York: Holt, Rinehart and Winston, 1962.

McKinney, F. *Counseling for Personal Adjustment*. Boston: Houghton Mifflin, 1958.

Patterson, C. H. *Counseling and Guidance in Schools*. New York: Harper & Row, 1962.

Pepinsky, H. and Pauline. *Counseling Theory and Practice.* New York: Ronald, 1954.

Reik, T. *Listening with the Third Ear.* New York: Farrar, Straus & Giroux, 1949.

Thorne, F. C. *Principles of Personality Counseling.* Brandon, Vt.: Journal of Clinical Psychology, 1950.

Tolbert, E. L. *Introduction to Counseling.* New York: McGraw-Hill, 1959.

Tyler, Leona. *The Work of the Counselor,* 2nd ed. New York: Appleton, 1961.

Williamson, E. G. *Counseling Adolescents.* New York: McGraw-Hill, 1950.

――――. *How to Counsel Students.* New York: McGraw-Hill, 1939.

――――, and Hahn, M. E. *Introduction to High School Counseling.* New York: McGraw-Hill, 1940.

Wolberg, L. *The Technique of Psychotherapy.* New York: Grune & Stratton, 1954.

Zerfoss, K. *Readings in Counseling.* New York: Association Press, 1952.

CHAPTER I   Psychology and Pastoral Care

1. Normatively speaking, pastoral theology also draws on history as one of its sources. Any study of spiritual direction should consider the traditional methods by which the task has always found, throughout the Church's history, its own working methods and its own means of expression, and has formulated its own goals. The importance of tradition in the formulation of pastoral doctrine was well emphasized by Paul Broutin, S.J., in his article "Histoire et tradition pastorales," *Nouvelle Revue Théologique,* 77, 7 (July 1955), pp. 725–736. Another important work by the same author should also yield useful information: *La Réforme pastorale en France au XVIIᵉ siècle,* 2 volumes, Paris-Tournai, Desclée et Cie., 1956; also, Father H. Bremond's *L'Histoire littéraire du sentiment religieux en France,* 12 volumes, Paris, Bloud et Gay, 1921–1933. English translation: *A Literary History of Religious Thought in France,* New York, Macmillan, 1928–1936. It remains true that a real history of spiritual direction has yet to be written, although

such a book would certainly mark a great step forward in the renewal of psychological methods in pastoral relations, normatively speaking. There is a great deal of useful material as well as many debatable interpretations in the book by John J. McNeill, A *History of the Cure of Souls*, New York, Harper & Row, 1951.

2. Canon S. Ligier, in the Introduction to his book *L'adulte des milieux ouvriers; essai de psychologie pastorale*, Paris, Éditions Ouvrières, 1950, provides an answer to the theory that the duality of sources (pastoral theology as a source of normative instructions and pastoral psychology as a source of scientific observations) will lead to the development of two separate, autonomous sciences. In the same book there is an interesting letter to the author from Father Y. Congar, from which we quote briefly: "Theology must be thought of as the living work of the believing mind. Possessing the unchangeable as it does, and having access to the highest sources, theology should be an eternal quest, it should call on science and technology, it should enlist any techniques which may help toward a truer knowledge of Christian reality. In the case you mention, it does all the work. It is a living branch of theology, not just a technical sociopsychological thesis in need of a few supernatural trimmings" (p. 29). Concerning the twofold foundation on which the development of a Spiritual Theology must rest, Father J. de Guibert is of the same opinion in his *Theologia Spiritualis*, 4th ed., Rome, Ed. Gregoriana, 1952, pp. 19–32. This work is available in English: *Theology of the Spiritual Life*, New York, Sheed & Ward, 1953.

3. Modern psychologists are vividly aware of the limitations of psychology as applied to the study of psychic functions and their determining factors. Many names could be cited in support of this, but we will mention only two: the classic work by Dr. Charles Odier, *Les deux sources, consciente et inconsciente, de la vie morale*, 2nd ed., Neuchâtel, Baconnière, 1943; and F. Duyckaerts' *La notion de normal en psychologie clinique*, Paris, Vrin, 1954.

4. Paul Ricoeur provides a remarkable demonstration of the concept of using determining factors as a category in order to

establish and understand the relationship between psychic phenomena and morality: "Infantile sexuality and adult morality may share the same affective potential. The origin of affective 'matter' and the meaning of intentional 'form' are two radically different problems. There is nothing scandalous in the psychoanalyst's discovery that the same affective matter lies at the roots of an entire discrete series of consciously experienced values, from the animal to the sacred." *Philosophie de la volonté*, Volume 1, pp. 380 ff., Paris, Aubier, 1949. Father A. Plé, O.P., has often discussed the relationship between this theme and thomist philosophy in the *Supplément de la Vie Spirituelle*. For example: *Saint Thomas et la psychologie des profondeurs* (November 15, 1952); *L'acte moral et la pseudo-morale de l'inconscient* (February 15, 1957); *La maturité affective: esquisse théologique* (September 15, 1958). For a psychological and phenomenological treatment of the psychic forces which oppose or unite men in the processes of identification and participation, see the important and sometimes (especially on a religious level) summary work of A. Hesnard, *Psychanalyse du lien interhumain*, Paris, Presses Universitaires de France, 1957.

5. In the same way, certain psychological interviewing techniques (here playing the role of "matter," even when scientifically handled) should be reconsidered from a pastoral viewpoint. It is quite possible that this new, specifically religious aim will have little effect on a given technique. It is equally possible that the technique will be radically altered and certain aspects of it rejected completely as unsuitable for pastoral goals. We are thinking here in particular of the human-relations techniques studied in the school of Carl Rogers; we have drawn heavily upon them, but we have always tried to rethink them in terms of the theologically defined aims of the pastoral relationship. Father D. H. Salman, O.P., was probably justified when he reproached Father Charles A. Curran (whose work is listed in its rightful place at the head of the Notes) for limiting himself too closely to Rogerian techniques in his attempts to improve pastoral counseling. Father Salman's criticism appeared in the *Supplément de la Vie Spirituelle*, November 15, 1953, pp. 469–475. Some of the techniques may be used, but we must think through them again and sometimes even go beyond

them. It is also worth remarking that almost all the counselees mentioned by Father Curran are involved in problems of morality unconnected with a strictly religious and Christian spiritual life. From this point of view, Seward Hiltner's is the better book.

6. The connection between scientific psychology and pastoral work is thus reduced to a twofold relationship: an extrinsic relationship, when it is a question of preaching the message of salvation or administering the sacraments, and an intrinsic relationship, when it is a question of an improved reception or expression of grace, a freely accepted gift of God, in order to diffuse it more thoroughly, both psychologically and socially. This theological solution was particularly well expressed in a study by Father Louis Beirnaert, S.J.: "La sanctification dépend-elle du psychisme?" *Études*, July 1950, pp. 58–65. This article was reprinted in *Expérience chrétienne et psychologie*, Paris, Éditions de l'Épi, 1964. An English translation, "Does Sanctification Depend Upon Psychic Structure?" appeared in *Cross Currents*, No. 2, Winter 1951, pp. 39–43. Recently the same author returned to the topic of techniques in announcing the Christian message (their uses and limitations): "Le conditionnement dans l'Église," *Études*, January 1961, pp. 3–15. An English translation, "The Problem of Conditioning in the Church," was published in *Readings in European Catechetics*, Brussels, Lumen Vitae Press, 1962, pp. 63–72.

7. The specificity of religious values is threatened in a far more insidious manner by a sort of "psychologism," or boasting, about the part played by Christianity in preserving or restoring mental health. This exaggerated viewpoint is expressed in complete good faith by some American promoters of the current movement for a "reconciliation" between psychiatry and members of the clergy. To quote two texts chosen at random from the *Academy Reporter* (the Bulletin of the Academy for Religious and Mental Health, New York): "A mentally healthy person should be able to act in the face of anxiety. Faith is a factor that enables people to do this." (IV, December 9, 1959, p. 3) "It is now widely recognized that he [the psychotherapist] not only does but should make value judgments . . . in relation to his patients. . . . Psychiatry leads the

individual to relinquish his narcissism, 'the sin of Lucifer,' and
gives him a deepening understanding of himself, helps him to accept others, and eventually gives him a sense of the community.
As for the spiritual values of therapy, there is the necessity
of resolving the problem of the relation of the individual to God,
the Giver of all." (V, February 2, 1960, p. 3) Religion thus becomes a trump card in the hand of the mental healer, and God is
seen as a means for assuring mental health; here, we would say, the
values seem upside down. Of course, this is not the viewpoint of
all the contributors of the *Academy Reporter*.

This confusion between psychic functions and Christian values is
not confined to the United States. In Ignace Lepp's *Hygiène de
l'âme*, Paris, Aubier, 1958, we find this deplorable preamble on "the
sick soul": "Ever since the beginning of history, man seems to have
experienced this sickness of the soul. Today, these illnesses are
conventionally referred to as neuroses or psychoses. They can be
cured by various psychotherapeutic treatments. . . ." Undoubtedly
the author is justified in his use of the term "conventional." But it
seems doubtful whether a Christian can use this "convention,"
abandoning his belief that the moral sickness of the soul is caused
by sin (and not neurosis) and accepting this lamentable confusion
between the soul and the psyche which must be protested, if only
in the interest of patients undergoing psychotherapy.

The basis of this question was thoroughly discussed from a
theological and psychotherapeutic viewpoint in a debate between
Father Louis Beirnaert and Doctor Wilfrid Daim: "Psychothérapie
et problème de Dieu," *Études*, January 1957, pp. 67–72, and July
1957, pp. 84–94. Certain humorous aggressiveness should not
distract the reader from the essential seriousness of this discussion
on both the speculative and practical levels. It is a question of the
specificity of Christian values in their articulation with the techniques of clinical psychology.

The teaching of Pope Pius XII on these necessary distinctions
should also be consulted, especially his speech of April 10, 1958,
"Applied Psychology." (An English translation was published by
the National Catholic Welfare Conference, 1312 Massachusetts
Avenue, N.W., Washington, D.C.)

Generally, Jewish pastoral work is careful to respect the transcendent nature of the pastoral function and its religious goals in

psychological work itself. This can be observed in a book by Louis Linn and Leo Schwarz, *Psychiatry and Religious Experience* (New York, Random House, 1958), also in the articles by Rabbi I. Fred Hollander, "The Specific Nature of the Clergy's Role in Mental Health" (*Pastoral Psychology*, November 1959, pp. 11–21), and by Professor Abraham N. Franzblau, "Distinctive Functions of Psychotherapy and Pastoral Counseling" (*Archives of General Psychiatry*, December 1960, pp. 583–589).

Finally, the problem of the psychotherapist and his patient sharing the same moral and religious values has been closely studied by Father L. Beirnaert, S.J.: "Est-il souhaitable qu'un croyant soit toujours analysé par un croyant?" with a discussion, in *Psyché*, No. 30, April 1949, pp. 358–367. See also, by the same author, "L'usage thérapeutique de la vie religieuse" in the collected reports of the Seventh International Catholic Congress of Clinical Psychology, *Conducta religiosa y salud mental*, Madrid, Olivos 18, 1957, pp. 175–179, and "Expérience spirituelle et psychothérapie," *Supplément de la Vie Spirituelle*, No. 56, February 15, 1961, pp. 111–118.

CHAPTER II   Psychological Functions of Pastoral Counseling

1. A much more profound analysis of the attitudes implicit in the unconditional acceptance of the counselee, in the genuine sharing in his vision of the world and of himself ("empathy"), and especially the application of these attitudes in a discussion of the actual answers and possible answers given at difficult moments during interviews is available in the book, already mentioned, by Carl Rogers and G. Marian Kinget: *Psychothérapie et relations humaines*. This work is thoroughly recommended, especially Volume II, *La Pratique*, to those wishing to improve the psychological quality of their interviews, as well as to circles or groups working along the same lines. The practical examples should be studied. In addition, other exercises should be worked out, based on real pastoral interviews or on situations proper to spiritual direction.

2. For an improved "supervision" of pastoral work, either individually or in groups, we are currently having to rely on methods already tested in the training of social workers (free, as we said, to transfer them to a pastoral perspective). In order to feel the "spirit" of these methods, some simple, relevant readings are available: "Compréhensions psychologique et Service Social," an article by Father Duyckaerts in *Service Social dans le Monde*, XII, October 4, 1953 (Brussels, 111 rue de la Poste); *Réflexions sur le Case-work*, Part III of *L'Ésquisse d'une psychologie de l'homme*, published in *Pages Documentaires*, No. 3, February 1954 (16, rue Tiphaine, Paris), with articles by Fathers Cruchon, Oraison, etc.; *Réflexions sur une expérience de formation à l'aide psycho-sociale*, also in *Pages Documentaires*, No. 2, December 1960, with articles by Fathers Beirnaert, Oraison, Miss Lehmann, etc. Also several articles by Father Beirnaert in *Études*: "Aide et dialogue," September 1961, pp. 173–181; "Formation au dialogue d'aide," June 1962, pp. 300–311. One could also include the article by Father J. Rombauts, O.P., "L'entretien pastoral," in *Évangéliser* (Brussels, Éditions Pensée Catholique), No. 95, March 1962, pp. 472–481.

3. The analytic methods developed in this and the following chapters are widely used for psychological dialogue training in existing schools of clinical psychology. As far as their application to religious counseling is concerned, we must say that we owe a special debt to the classic work by Seward Hiltner, *Pastoral Counseling*, New York, Abingdon Press, 1949. Starting from examples borrowed from Hiltner, we have sometimes suggested that the members of our "pastoral psychology seminars" give their reactions and opinions, which are broadly reflected in the example analyzed in this chapter. They have always found Hiltner's basic material to be incomparably sound.

4. Concerning the considerate silence and its value in psychological welcome, research has shown that inexperienced counselors talk three times as much as the counselee (300 words for every 100). But experienced counselors often manage to say less than a quarter of all the words spoken—and recorded—in the course of a conversation (25 words in every 100). Naturally, this is a question

of the means employed. A point worth noting is that the counselors who say the least and ask the least number of precise questions are the ones who obtain the greatest quantity of really important data on the problem in question in the same space of time. The counselee knows his real problem far better than the counselor; once welcomed and reassured, he will move rapidly toward it. See also Carl Rogers, *Counseling and Psychotherapy*. Of course, in psychotherapeutic relations, the number of statements by the psychologist falls even lower than the proportions cited above.

5. Jean [4] concluded her remarks on the life of faith purged of its affective substrata by asking:

But do you think that might be what has happened to me? That I must go through this . . . almost mystical experience? One of our correspondents made the following observation concerning a possible reply: "It seems to me that a simple reflection is not called for here, because she is asking a question. But this doesn't necessarily mean an immediate reply. Better to let her search for one with us. I would suggest something like this:

"You seem to have found yourself in this situation which you thought remarkable. Yet you still seem a little afraid of it." It will now be up to her to explain what she means by "almost mystical," and it will not be necessary to hazard a guess at the answer.

6. A psychologically egocentric attitude finds expression in the frequent use of the pronoun "I" at the beginning of verbal replies, without any accompanying acceptance of genuinely experienced emotion. In fact, the systematic research mentioned in the text concerns conversations between neurotic patients in therapy. Their progress is accompanied by a fuller acceptance of subjectively experienced emotions and the reappearance of an ability to share the feelings of others; in other words, affective egocentricity is reduced. See the research, already mentioned, of Carl Rogers and William Snyder. Similar techniques have yet to be applied to the answers of pastoral counselors, but there seems to be no doubt about the probable statistical outcome: the frequency of the opening "I" accompanies a certain psychic or affective indisposition which makes the establishment of a sound psychological relationship

highly unlikely. Of course, the Christian charity of the pastoral counselor is not questioned here, any more than his good will or his moral availability to his counselees. It is just a question of their actual expression in the dialogue on the level of human relations, psychologically experienced and lived. For our part, after ten years of psychological work among the clergy, we are convinced that, taken as a whole, they are much more "open" in a moral and Christian sense than the analysis of their actual replies in the dialogue might lead one to believe. This, of course, is one reason for their desire to perfect the psychological aspect of their pastoral work.

7. The yearning to meet, in the course of this life, a representative of the "judge by whom all men would be judged," or to project a psychically equivalent image of him is a theme treated by Professor E. De Greeff in his posthumous work *L'homme et son juge*, Desclée De Brouwer, 1962. But the expression itself occurs in his novel: *Le juge Maury*, Paris, Éditions du Seuil, 1955, pp. 148 and 313.

8. The tendency of some spiritual directors to accept vows of obedience from their penitents quite readily, together with the rare occasions when it is advisable to accept such a vow, are discussed in: "Le voeu d'obéissance au Directeur," by Father Gabriel, in *Direction Spirituelle et Psychologie*, one volume of the *Études Carmélitaines*, Desclée De Brouwer, 1951, pp. 129–156. On the other hand, the *Rivista di Vita Spirituale* (Rome), V, July 3, 1951, published an interesting survey carried out among many theologians and spiritual directors concerning the relationship of "meekness" or "obedience" as it occurs in spiritual direction. The resulting opinions are not completely unanimous, but they do tend toward the idea that obedience, properly speaking, should be excluded from the psychological relationship in spiritual direction, although the value of meekness should be maintained. Certainly, a free consent to the director, when practiced in the spirit of faith, can be understood as a fruit of the virtue of prudence and a symbolic means of surrender to God.

9. The second fundamental function of pastoral dialogue covers two kinds of activity which Americans distinguish as "guidance" and "counseling." According to Charles Curran, the "guidance" relationship involves the giving of pertinent information on moral, religious, or ordinary social principles as they apply to an immediate, personal situation. The "counseling" relationship aims at enabling the counselee to think through his emotional difficulties and personal conflicts and in this way aids him to make a more adequate adjustment to them, always bearing his own moral principles in mind. This twofold activity of the correctly fulfilled pastoral function is extremely important for making sure that the counselee's motivation matures in a moral and Christian fashion. But the counseling technique is also at work in the first function (welcome), although in our opinion they are not totally identical when it is a question of pastoral counseling.

10. Concerning the third fundamental function, it must be pointed out that in a Christian perspective the priest is definitely a mediator and not a simple intermediary. His mission complete, the intermediary stops work and disappears. Mediation continues even after its goal has been achieved. This is why Christ is called the mediator and not the intermediary between God and men. The same is true of the work of the Church and her priests from both the sacramental and the strictly pastoral points of view. Thus the necessary withdrawal of the spiritual counselor should be understood as taking place on the psychic or affective levels of the relationship. On the plane of faith, symbolically experienced in the relationship, the spiritual, mediatory bond remains effective. Even in the spiritual direction of people who have received special grace and even a mystical type of enlightenment, the priest continues in his mediatory role, either as a counselor or as the representative of ecclesiastical authority.

Concerning the apparent contradiction between the unique mediation of Christ and the multiple "mediators" in the Church, see the solution offered by St. Thomas in the *Summa Theologica*, III, q. 26, art. I: priests, like prophets are only mediators *secundum quid* (relatively), *ministerialiter* (as servants), and *dispositive* (preparing the ground).

In the absence of a history of spiritual direction in Catholic tradition, it would be worth while to study the Protestant ideas on the function of mediation in pastoral dialogue. Jean-Daniel Benoît provides excellent, if somewhat polemic, material (emphasizing contrasts) in: *Direction spirituelle et protestantisme: étude sur la légitimité d'une direction protestante,* Paris, Alcan, 1940. Four recent works should make interesting comparisons. On the extreme right of pastoral austerity stands E. Thurneysen, *Doctrine de la cure de l'âme,* Neuchatel and Paris, Delachaux, 1958. English translation: *Theology of Pastoral Care,* Richmond, Va., John Knox Press, 1962. For this author, no portion of pastoral dialogue has any significance save as a vehicle for that divine, all-transcending Word: the forgiveness of sins. At the other extreme stands Carroll A. Wise, author of *Pastoral Counseling: Its Theory and Practice,* New York, Harper & Row, 1951. In this book the psychological nuances of the interpersonal relationship are minutely analyzed according to the symbolic role they are capable of playing in effecting the counselee's complete cure and liberation. It is not always clear, however, whether we are on the psychic or spiritual plane. A more balanced view, in our opinion, is provided by Seward Hiltner in his *Preface to Pastoral Theology,* 1958, and *Pastoral Counseling,* 1949, New York, Abingdon Press. Here the symbolic function and the objective role are happily combined, in respect to what a thomist philosopher would call analogical relations and progress. Finally, there is an extremely sound theological basis to the psychological theories of Wayne E. Oates in *Protestant Pastoral Counseling,* Philadelphia, Westminster Press, 1962, especially the remarkable chapter "The Holy Spirit as Counselor."

11. The question of the different planes and the analogical relationship also applies when considering psychologically experienced and morally recognized "guilt." It must now be made quite clear that the principal immediate function of confession is not to relieve man of his burden of psychic guilt but to bring about the mysterious, sacramental, and efficacious meeting with the objective forgiveness of God, in which effectiveness has no connection whatsoever with any sense of psychological release that may result from it. It is true that this sacramental action has only an extrinsic relationship with psychic determinism, while the priest in his pastoral work (spiritual direction, for example) is in close contact with it,

even when the dialogue concerns moral or religious problems. Thus it is possible for a priest, even though speaking words of encouragement or absolution, to increase the affective insecurity of a penitent simply by a reflection in the dialogue of the insufficiently developed or controlled personality of the priest. The *"Supplément de la Vie Spirituelle* devoted an entire issue (No. 61, May 15, 1962) to the biblical, theological, and psychological aspects of guilt, including one particularly profound speculative study: "La Pénitence, vertu de la culpabilité chrétienne," by Father J. M. Pohier, pp. 331–384. About the religious analogy latent in any psychotherapy, see a discussion between Thomas C. Oden and A. Godin in *Continuum* (New York, Herder, summer 1964 and winter 1965).

CHAPTER III   Human Mediation in Pastoral Dialogue

1. The statements by François Mauriac and Paul Claudel concerning the priest's role are taken from: *Qu'attendez-vous du prêtre?* edited by Daniel-Rops, Paris, Plon, 1949.

2. Even in the case of a psychiatric hospital chaplain, the fundamental aim of pastoral relations is not to procure sound therapeutic effects but to help the patient understand the message of salvation, taking his unhappy condition as a point of departure. Here is how Father Henri Bissonier puts it in "Qu'est-ce qu'un aumônier d'hôpital psychiatrique?": "The chaplain with a solid grounding in psychopathology will be able to distinguish healthy, positive elements behind the symptoms of the patient's disease, even if they are aggressive and apparently irreconcilable. . . . Using all that is whole and alive within himself, the patient grapples with evil, facing up to its threats, and struggling to rebuild with the debris of the destruction around him. . . . As a priest, he polarizes respect which might turn into fear, love which might become worship, or hatred which might provoke aggression. . . . But he is always heading toward God, with whom he is constantly trying to put the patient in contact. Now, the primary aim of this relationship is not therapeutic—it first makes sure that the sick man fulfills his one fundamental vocation: to know, love, and serve God." (*Humaniser l'hôpital psychiatrique*, Paris, Éditions du Cerf, 1958, pp. 92 and 96.)

An answer to the appeal made by God to all men of good faith cannot help being anything but beneficial to moral equilibrium and, indirectly, to mental health. It is all the more important, therefore, that the divine message should be correctly enunciated and understood with as few misinterpretations as possible. In this respect, provided the representatives of Christian values (priests, doctors, and psychiatric assistants) are careful to present them in their full purity and do not worry themselves unduly (unless specially qualified to do so) about any possible psychic advantages, then these values should favor the maturation and recovery of the psychic apparatus. Similarly, intellectually prudent and emotionally rich parents have a beneficial effect on the psychic condition of their children, provided they do not worry unduly about psychology. "Seek first the kingdom of God and the rest will be given to you in addition."

3. Cultural and social influences are obviously extremely important in structuring the priest's role and the projected image of his functions. Even within the Catholic church, and within the same culture, there are considerable variations in what counselees expect of the priest. Father Emile Pin, S.J., has shown that in the same parish in the same French town, religion and its representative, the priest, are expected to act as a powerful agent for social justice by the proletariat and workers; serve as a guarantee of salvation in the next life by the middle classes; and, finally, the leisured classes hope for the founding of little fraternal groups, rising above professional differences and urban boundaries. (*Pratique religieuses et classes sociales*, Paris, Spes, 1956, pp. 395–408.) Besides these variations due to different cultural or social origins, there are others depending on the age or sex of the counselee. This is a question which deserves closer attention and scientific study. Further details may be found in a study entitled *L'image du prêtre et de son rôle* in this author's book on religious psychology: *Le Dieu des parents et le Dieu des enfants* (Tournai and Paris, Casterman, 1963).

4. The pastoral relationship is influenced by various circumstances: authority, comradeship, competence, prestige, charm, hostility, lack of time, etc., which are well analyzed in a minor but

shrewdly suggestive work by Seward Hiltner: *The Counselor in Counseling*, New York, Abingdon Press, 1952.

5. The actual gravity of transference distortion in pastoral relations may vary tremendously. At this point we make no attempt to distinguish a genuine neurotic transference from one which might even be called normal. This might, for example, result from a young counselee's psychic or spiritual immaturity when faced with the priestly role, or be caused by socially structured and possibly dangerous images shared by the majority of adults in a given environment, even a Christian one. As for pathological transferences and the distinction between neuroses and psychoses, these were discussed in detail in this author's *Guide (à l'usage du clergé) pour discerner les troubles mentaux*, 2nd ed., Brussels, Éditions Oeuvre des Tracts (184, rue Washington), 1962. We believe that the "pastoral resolution" of a true neurotic transference will be relatively rare unless appropriate treatment has been undertaken elsewhere. This is even more true of psychotic patients. But this should not prevent the priest from acting as a "religious mediator" before, during, and after the treatment, whether this is successful or not.

6. Father Beirnaert treats the problem of distinguishing between "infantilism" and a "childlike spirit" in the same sentence: "Spiritual infancy is a permanent creative state, while infantilism does nothing but repeat past reactions." (*La Vie Spirituelle*, a special issue devoted to *Enfance et Maturité spirituelles*, October 1951, Paris, Éditions du Cerf, p. 303.) As Father Oraison says: "One cannot really be as a child before God unless one is sufficiently adult before men." (*Devant l'illusion et l'angoisse*, Paris, Fayard, 1958, p. 168.)

7. An exceptionally relevant pastoral study concerning the spiritual direction of women appeared in the *Supplément de la Vie Spirituelle*, May 1950, No. 13, pp. 123–150. Entitled "La direction spirituelle des femmes" by Henri Sauvage, a slightly abridged version was reprinted in *Notes de Pastorale familiale* (Brussels, Éditions des Feuilles Familiales), X, 5 (May and June 1961.) An excellent essay by Ida F. Görres is available in German: "Einige Erwägungen über die Begegnung des Priesters mit der Frau," in

his excellent book *Laien-Gedanken zum Zölibat*, Frankfurt, Knecht Verlag, 1962. A French translation, *Sur le célibat des prêtres*, was published by the Éditions du Cerf, Paris, 1963.

An article by J. Trouslard should be read concerning difficulties encountered by certain priests when dealing with members of the managerial or intellectual classes: *Le prêtre et les milieux indépendants*, Brochure No. 728 in the series *Études religieuses*, Brussels, Éditions de la Pensée Catholique, 1957, in which the author provides a vivid account of his problems without helping to resolve them. Other aspects of this type of pastoral work are dealt with in the special issue, May 1959, of *Evangeliser* (Brussels) entitled *Pastorale des milieux indépendants*. Also by Joseph Comblin, *Échec de l'Action Catholique?* Paris, Éditions Universitaires, 1961, who points out that many of the priests who pass their time in youth movements often lack the necessary maturity to face typically adult problems, especially in industrial, political, scientific, or artistic circles which have developed beyond the reach of any form of Christianity. He shows that only the work of Father Teilhard de Chardin has affected this intellectual climate, in scientific circles at least. Seward Hiltner's *The Christian Shepherd: Some Aspects of Pastoral Care*, New York, Abingdon Press, 1959, offers a richly suggestive perspective of pastoral work among the managerial classes. The situations described in this book are typically American.

8. The following works should be read as an introduction to pastoral work among elderly people: "Religion and the Aging" by Louis Linn and Leo Schwarz in *Psychiatry and Religious Experience*, New York, Random House, 1958; *Older People and the Church* by P. B. Maves and J. L. Cedarleaf, New York, Abingdon Press, 1949; and *How to Help Older People* by J. K. Arthur, Philadelphia, Lippincott, 1954, a much more secular work. We have been unable to find anything in French in this neglected field. Yet the elderly, considered from the twofold perspective of full human reality and the reality of faith, are surely those who come closest to that fulfillment of human destiny which is the prerogative of "the new man." For a phenomenological and theological point of view, see several chapters in two books by Father Roger Troisfontaines: *Je ne meurs pas . . .* (1960), English translation, *I Do Not Die*, New York, Desclée, 1963; and *J'entre dans la vie*, Paris, Éditions

Universitaires, 1963. Also his article "Le sens de la destinée terrestre," in *Revue Nouvelle*, Brussels, March 15, 1959, pp. 253–263.

9. Should the real nature of transference and its general psychic effects on pastoral dialogue become a subject for study? Even those who advocate a psychological renewal in the catachumenate and pastoral work are not unanimous on this subject. Thus, in an excellent pamphlet published by Father François Coudreau ("Simples conseils aux catéchistes d'adultes," in *Vérité et Vie*, Strasbourg, January 1960, 45, No. 363), the author discusses the necessary conditions for receiving adult catachumens. He suggests that we concentrate on: 1) the actual state of the counselee's religious knowledge; 2) his interior psychological and spiritual attitudes, these being indicative of either a moral openness or of a door closed in the face of Christian faith and values.

In our opinion, this twofold approach, with which all pastoral dialogue should be primarily and essentially concerned, does not cover the entire relationship as established between the priest and his counselee. The relationship itself is pushed to one side, so to speak, and there is also a grave risk of confusing moral and psychological attitudes.

This additional examination of the psychic or affective forces involved does not excuse us from examining the counselee's religious knowledge and his moral attitudes; indeed, it will help us to examine them much better.

Perhaps all examination of psychic influences should be reserved for "difficult cases" or for the correction of pastoral values which cannot be otherwise explained. Granted that this examination is not absolutely essential in every case, we do not feel that these psychic influences are at all unusual.

This point of view is adopted, wisely it seems to us, in a book which has already been mentioned, by G. Hagmaier and R. Gleason, *Counseling the Catholic*, in which the authors insist on the particular nature of the transference relation in the pastoral care of the scrupulous and other reputedly "difficult" types of person: alcoholics, homosexuals, etc. They never lose sight of the religious goal (not merely the moral or educative one) to be aimed at, even if therapy should prove unsuccessful.

10. A balance must be maintained between religious aims, the observation of psychological processes at work in the counselee and, in particular, an awareness of variations in his relationship with the priest in pastoral dialogue. This will be found in three articles which we thoroughly recommend for reading in depth:

D. H. Salman, O.P. "Psychologie moderne et direction morale," in *Supplément de la Vie Spirituelle* (Paris, Éditions du Cerf), No. 38, September 15, 1956, pp. 262–278.

N. Mailloux, O.P. "Psychologie pastorale et problèmes de la direction de conscience," Volume IV of *Contributions à l'étude des sciences de l'homme* (Montreal, Éditions de la Librairie Dominicaine), 1959, pp. 66–130.

Dr. G. Mora. "Quelques aspects du transfert chez les scrupuleux," in *Supplément de la Vie Spirituelle*, No. 36, February 15, 1956, pp. 81–98.

11. When we speak of a characteristic psychotherapeutic technique in which transference is increased in order that it may be later reduced—a technique quite unsuitable for the pastoral relationship—we are referring to the psychoanalysis-inspired psychotherapies. According to his disciples, the techniques of Carl Rogers result in a reduction of any transference elements which may be present in the counselee's initial attitude. This point is clearly explained by G. M. Kinget (*op. cit.*), Volume II, Chapter VI, "Transfert et diagnostic."

12. When, on the other hand, we say that one characteristic of pastoral dialogue is to accept the initial degree of transference and explain its symbolic significance, eventually arriving at its spiritual value on the plane of faith and that this method is unsuitable for use in psychotherapeutic dialogue as such, then we are considering things from the point of view of a technique based on affective dynamisms, psychoanalytic as well as Rogerian. "Value" discussions are permitted and even encouraged in some recent psychotherapy methods ("logotherapy" and "existential therapy": Frankl, Daim, etc.). Here we will merely refer the reader to the discussion between Dr. W. Daim and Father Beirnaert in *Études*, January and July 1957.

The author has already discussed the distinctive characteristics of pastoral dialogue, comparing them with those proper to psycho-therapeutic dialogue in "Action thérapeutique et action pastorale," *Supplément de la Vie Spirituelle*, No. 44, February 15, 1958, pp. 21–30.

13. "The veiled symbol is transformed into a symbolic veil." We have always considered this expression of Father René Thibaut, S.J., in *Le sens de l'Homme-Dieu*, 2nd ed., Brussels, Éditions Universelles, 1946, as being of immense theological and pastoral significance. On the one hand—and especially for moderns, Christ's suffering human nature appears as a veil concealing his divinity; then, when viewed with the eyes of faith (so much more easily by us, imbued as we are with Christian values), it becomes the most expressive symbol of divine charity. Thus when the relationship with the priest is encumbered by a transference, sometimes making a mockery of his priestly role, it remains a veil and an obstacle on the pastoral plane until the moment when this veil itself is seen, with eyes of faith, to be the greatest possible symbol of the priestly and pastoral relationships: "being all things for all people," and "be there not to be served but to serve."

14. The process described under the heading "The growth of scrupulosity based on unconscious aggression" is not to be taken as a prototype for pastoral work among the scrupulous. According to a remarkable article by Father N. Mailloux, O.P. (*Supplément de la Vie Spirituelle*, No. 39, November 15, 1956, pp. 425–439), there are at least four different psychic fields which feed the phenomena of scrupulosity: *Anxiety* (panic or uncontrollable fear when confronted with the mere possibility of temptation, sin or having to make the simplest decision: moral phobia); *Obsession-compulsion* (often based on shame: the growth of ritualistic patterns, actions, and precautions which soon replace the concern for true morality); *Compulsive self-accusation* (a desire to be humiliated, punished, or reprimanded: the same accusations are repeated over and over again, right down to the last, most insignificant detail); *Suppressed aggression* (pathological mistrust: everything has already been tried and found wanting—nobody can enlighten "my" conscience . . .). The reader will have realized that the process discussed here belongs in the fourth category. In any of the other categories, the

attitude adopted by the counselor would not have had the slightest chance of success.

Father Henri Gratton, O.M.I., provides some clear and instructive remarks in "La psychologie pastorale du scrupule," in *Supplément de la Vie Spirituelle*, No. 48, February 15, 1959, pp. 95–123. Also worth reading are A. Lauras and C. Larere, "Obsessions et scrupules: psychiatrie et pastorale," in the *Cahiers Laënnec*, 1960, No. 2 (June), pp. 67–78 (Lethielleux).

15. "Complete self-knowledge as a human being must involve an awareness that one is *dependent* upon sensory conditions and yet is free within symbolic relationships." This forceful expression of Madame F. Dolto-Marette comes from her article "Acquisition de l'autonomie," in *Limites de l'Humain, Études Carmélitaines*, Desclée De Brouwer, 1953, p. 137. It summarizes the philosophical basis of the positions adopted in Chapter III concerning the pastoral treatment of transference. Neurotic or not, the counselee need not feel ashamed at recognizing the psychic processes which lead to the opening of the pastoral dialogue and ensure its continuance. The transference condition, with its affective (individual) or cultural origins, serves as a basis for a liberating process which will itself receive powerful support from the religious, Christian symbolisms which illuminate and reveal the ultimate end of our existence, a loving opening of the heart to the spoken word of God, as well as the ultimate significance of the pastoral relationship itself.

CHAPTER IV   One Method of Improvement

1. The Apostolic Constitution "Sedes Sapientiae" (May 31, 1956) included the following remarks on the training and instruction of priests: "It is absolutely essential that future pastors should receive instruction from competent teachers in accordance with the teachings of the Holy See concerning the latest developments in psychology and pedagogy, in didactics and catechetics, and in social, pastoral, and similar fields. This will train them to meet the multiple demands of the modern apostolate. . . . So-called practical instruction should also be included which should be carefully con-

ducted and wisely supervised." (*Acta Apostolica Sedis*, 48, 1956, p. 364.) A French translation is available in *Documentation Catholique* (Paris), V. 53, Col. 860.

Moreover, the Apostolic Constitution "Ad Uberrima" (June 3, 1958) included the following subjects in a suggested two-year specialized-study course: religious sociology and "pastoral statistics"; individual and group spiritual direction; education and educational psychology; pastoral psychiatry. (*Acta Apostolica Sedis*, 50, 1958, p. 463.)

2. An excellent over-all view of the training of priests in pastoral psychology is given in *Pastoral Care and Clinical Training* by H. Faber, published by the (Protestant) Research Center in Religious Sociology and Pastoral Psychology (Leiden, Holland), Van Loghum Slaterus, Arnhem, 1961. The question is considered under three aspects: courses as part of the normal curriculum; specialized training courses in pastoral psychology; and training methods suitable for priests already in pastoral work.

a) Concerning courses to be introduced into the normal curriculum, it seems that they could probably be given during philosophy and theology, and should be divided into three parts. Lessons in (applied) religious psychology will describe the general constants of religious development, based on the same processes that govern personality growth; they will also deal with the part played by the pastor in the establishment and growth of the bond of faith in the individual Christian or nonbeliever. A second part will be devoted to religious social psychology and will prepare the way for a thorough study of the work of priests among different groups, e.g., the Sunday-morning congregation, parish societies, and study groups. Finally, a short course on psychopathology in pastoral work will describe diagnostic criteria, the attitudes to be developed, and the means to be used for referring the mentally ill to the appropriate specialists.

The spirit in which this training is given should be quite different from the erudite lectures and theoretical discussions which may be essential in specialized courses. Constant reference should be made to the experience gained in the role *already* played by priests, while insisting that attempts be made, as always, to do it more methodically, more effectively, and in greater security.

Religion and Mental Health: A Catholic Viewpoint is the title of a thirty-six page booklet (1960), edited by Father Vincent V. Herr, S.J., Director of Loyola University's (Chicago) Religion and Mental Health Project, Academy of Religion and Mental Health, 16 East 34 Street, New York. It describes a somewhat ambitious project for the scientific observation of the effects on young Catholic priests of the introduction into their theology curriculum of an intensive course given by a priest-psychiatrist (the late Father W. J. Devlin, S.J.), consisting of fifteen days of study and group work. This pilot study is extremely important for the development of this type of curriculum in American Catholic seminaries. It also includes a detailed outline of the role and functions of the Catholic priest in the mental-health field. The techniques used and the tests and the statistical results are available in the *Journal of Social Psychology*, 1961, 55, pp. 245–251, described by N. J. Webb and F. J. Kobler: "Clinical-Empirical Techniques for Assessing the Attitudes of Religious Towards Psychiatry."

The outline of a course given by Seward Hiltner ("Religion and Personality," 1959), with a list of lectures, personal work projects, and an original formula used in the final examination may be found in H. Faber's *Pastoral Care and Clinical Training, op. cit.* pp. 110–121.

A detailed program for a five-session course on pastoral psychology is also suggested by Ernest E. Bruder: "Clinical Pastoral Training in Preparation for the Pastoral Ministry," in *Journal of Pastoral Care*, XVI, 1, Spring 1962, pp. 25–33. For a Jewish point of view on this question, see Fred Hollander, "The Specific Nature of the Clergy's Role," in *Pastoral Psychology*, X, 98, November 1959, pp. 11–21.

b) *A specialized training program.* The Association Medico-psychologique d'aide aux Religieux, 18, rue des Tanneries, Paris XIII, is developing a specialized one-year training program which will qualify priests by means of constant supervision for specialized work, e.g., the chaplaincy of a psychiatric hospital; the spiritual direction of neurotics; the perception of vocational contra-indications, and similar difficulties encountered in the religious life. The standards adopted for the clinical pastoral training by the National Conference on Clinical Pastoral Training (Protestant), together with a course and supervision plan, are given in H. Faber's *Pastoral Care and Clinical Training, op. cit.*, pp. 41–46.

A teacher giving a basic course in pastoral counseling might use (apart from the works by Curran, Hiltner, and Gleason-Hagmaier, mentioned in Note 1): Paul E. Johnson, *Pastoral Ministration*, London, Nisbet, 1955. An American edition of the same author's *Psychology of Pastoral Care* was published in 1953 by the Abingdon Press, New York. He will find much worth-while descriptive information, together with accounts of actual cases and situations, in the three following works: *Casebook in Pastoral Counseling* (edited by N. S. Cryer and J. M. Vayhinger), New York and Nashville, Abingdon Press, 1962; *Religion and Mental Health: A Casebook with Commentary and an Essay on Pertinent Literature* by Hans Hoffmann, New York, Harper & Row, 1961; *The Minister's Consultation Clinic* (edited by Simon Doniger), Great Neck, New York, Channel Press, 1955.

Concerning the over-all problem of the integration of a minimal (or maximal) working knowledge of pastoral psychology into the theological curriculum, one would do well to read a report on the April, 1961, Evanston meeting by S. Hiltner and J. H. Ziegler, "Clinical Pastoral Education and the Theological Schools," in *Journal of Pastoral Care*, XV, 3 (Fall 1961), pp. 129–143.

3. Concerning the historical reasons which led pastoral psychology in the United States toward problems connected with mental hygiene (the prevention and cure of mental illness) and to collaboration with psychiatrists and psychologists, see H. Faber, *Pastoral Care and Clinical Training, op. cit.* The movement seems to spring from a profound desire to help mental patients on the level of their potential human and religious contacts with members of the clergy (hospital chaplains). In Chapter V, the author provides a sound critical commentary on the advantages and disadvantages which, as a result of this inspiration, have affected the development of pastoral psychology in the United States.

A descriptive study, copiously documented and illustrated by several methical surveys, is provided by Richard V. McCann, *The Churches and Mental Health*, New York, Basic Books, 1962. It includes some important psychosocial conclusions: A survey taken among 2,460 people in 1960 showed that 14% had visited a counselor at some time during their life for help with their affective or psychological problems and that 42% of these had turned to members of the clergy (*op. cit.*, p. 69). The majority of the

235,000 active members of the clergy are at least occasionally involved with people suffering from mental disorders, but only 8,000 of them can be considered as having received a *minimal* amount of instruction in clinical or psychiatric types of pastoral psychology (*op. cit.*, p. 81). Carefully and precisely, the author describes the reactions of the three main religions (Catholics, Protestants, and Jews) to this situation, also the current tendencies toward psychological training during theological studies, in improvement sessions, and in specialized centers. Finally he discusses the possibilities of human and religious action provided by contacts made by hospital chaplains with their patients on the one hand and with the doctors on the other. This book is part of a study commissioned by The Congress of the United States on July 28, 1955, to be conducted by the "Joint Commission on Mental Illness and Health." The study was originated by Kenneth E. Appel, in association with Leo H. Bartemeier. The report of the commission was completed on March 23, 1961.

In French, a descriptive study is available by J. C. Blumen and A. W. Eister: "Conseillers confessionnels et conseillers professionels autour de la psychologie pastorale," in *Archives de Sociologie des Religions* (Paris, No. 7, January-June 1959, pp. 131–143). A strong contrast is drawn between the image of the spiritual counselor and his role as seen by Protestant clergymen, by Catholic priests, and by professionals in the field of psychological relations: psychologists, doctors, and social workers.

4. Concerning the organization and supervision of courses in hopsital or parish work, designed to improve the training of young members of the clergy, see Chapter III in H. Faber's *Pastoral Care and Clinical Training, op. cit.* Another essay by David M. Taylor describes the situation in Australia (*Journal of Pastoral Care*, XVI, 1, Spring 1962, pp. 34–40). There is a short report by William E. Hulme on the work being done among English Lutherans (*Pastoral Psychology*, October 1959, p. 20). Finally, special attention should be paid to the descriptions by S. Hiltner in *Pastoral Counseling* (New York, Abingdon Press, 1949, Notes 1 to 6 of Chapter X, pp. 283–285), in *Clinical Pastoral Training* (New York, Federal Council of Churches of Christ in America, 1945), and in "Clinical Pastoral Education and the Theological Schools" (*Journal of Pastoral Care*, XV, 3, Fall 1961, pp. 129–143.)

Information concerning the organization of supervised pastoral psychology work in hospitals is contained in two articles by the Rev. Ernest E. Bruder. The first deals with the training of specialist chaplains: "Training and the Mental Hospital Chaplain," in *Journal of Pastoral Care*, XI, 3, Fall 1957, pp. 136–145. The second deals with the introduction of future pastors to human relations in pastoral work: "Clinical Pastoral Training in Preparation for the Pastoral Ministry," in *Journal of Pastoral Psychology*, XVI, 1, Spring 1962, pp. 25–33. An attempt at a technical evaluation of this type of training was provided and described by John Rea Thomas ("Evaluation of Clinical Pastoral Training and 'Part-Time' Training in a General Hospital," in *Journal of Pastoral Psychology*, XII, Spring 1958, pp. 28–38.

Several Catholic institutions in the United States have had extensive experience of supervised hospital courses for some priests (psychology students and future psychiatric hospital chaplains). Some students from the Catholic University of America, in Washington, take courses in St. Elizabeth's Hospital, the Seton Institute, Baltimore (Dr. Bartemeier), and in other institutions under the supervision of Fathers John W. Stafford, C.S.V., and Wilbur F. Wheeler (see Richard V. McCann, *op. cit.*, pp. 114–115).

Father W. W. Meissner, S.J., has described a program at St. Elizabeth's Hospital in Washington which is designed to introduce theology students to different problems connected with mental illness and interpersonal relationships, using the psychological and pastoral experience of the chaplain ("Psychiatric Training for Theology Students: A Report," in *The Psychiatric Quarterly* (State Hospital Press, Utica, New York), 35 (1961), pp. 720–725. Each session lasts for nine full days, and there is one session every fifteen days from September to December. The day begins with a lecture and a demonstration interview with a patient. Then each member has two and a half hours of direct contact with the patients. Psychiatric records may be consulted in the hospital office, always under a doctor's supervision. The day ends with another lecture given by a specialist, followed by a discussion period. An evaluation of each student's attitude is attempted at the beginning and end of the course.

There can be no doubt that this is a particularly effective method of providing theology students with a considerable degree of maturity in human relations; it also prompts them into a more personal assimilation of the theology courses themselves.

Although pastoral contacts in hospitals may provide an excellent foundation for training in clinical and in pastoral psychology, psychological training cannot be completed without some sort of supervised relations under normal parish conditions. In the absence of true individual supervision, this work-study has been assured by the *Centre de Formation Pastorale et Missionnaire* (35, rue de la Glacière, Paris XIII; Father F. J. Bonduelle, O.P.). This is probably one of the finest applications of that final year of pastoral training, required since 1956 for all priests and religious by the Apostolic Constitution *Sedes Sapientiae*, with the *General Statutes* of the Sacred Congregation for Religious (1957—Heading XI, art. 51–53), although this does not seem to have been successfully applied in many countries.

5. If the practice of supervised courses is already quite widespread among American Protestants, the Catholics seem to have made a greater use of intensive sessions, summer courses, and specialized institutes and seminars in an effort to improve the quality of their priests and nuns as psychological counselors. The subjects discussed by the lecturer, the timetable used, and the style adopted in the discussion groups are given in the published accounts of these meetings.

The Comité Permanent des Religieux de France (Father J. F. Barbier, O.F.M., 7, rue Marie-Rose, Paris IV) has organized a series of annual specialized sessions designed for Novice Masters, Prefects of Studies, Junior Seminary Directors, and Superiors. The conferences given at these sessions were published in the following numbers of the *Supplément de la Vie Spirituelle:* 52 (February 15, 1960), 56 (February 15, 1961), 60 (February 15, 1962), and 64 (February 15, 1963).

The pastoral training sessions devoted to problems of mental health, organized at St. John's University, Collegeville, Minnesota, by Fathers Alexius Portz and Gordon Tavis, O.S.B. (three or four sessions are held each summer for clergy of all denominations) have resulted in several brochures, dealing mainly with discussions recorded during the evening "symposium," based on a given text. For example: *Working Relationships Between Pastor and Psy-*

chiatrist (1956), *Religion, Psychiatry and Mental Health* (1957), *Immature Manifestations of Moral Conscience* (1958), *A Pastor's Relation to the Mentally Sick* (1960). Collegeville, Minn.: Institute for Mental Health.

A report by Father Kilian McDonnell, O.S.B., "Psychiatrie et Pastorale: une expérience de collaboration," in *Research in Religious Psychology* (Brussels, Lumen Vitae Press, 1957), pp. 57–63, should be read concerning the working *spirit* during these sessions.

A fine example of an intensive session (six days from 9 A.M. to 6:30 P.M.) organized for thirty theologians by the doctors and psychologists at the Menninger Foundation, Topeka, Kansas, is described by Harold C. Bradley, S.J. in "Une session de psychologie pastorale," *Supplement de la Vie Spirituelle*, No. 62, September 15, 1962, pp. 516–520.

The conferences given at the Institute for the Clergy on Problems in Pastoral Psychology, organized every two years at Fordham University by Father W. Bier, S.J., have been published in two volumes which we also recommend to teachers planning the subject matter for their pastoral psychology courses: *Problems in Pastoral Psychology* (a selection of the best lectures given in 1955 and 1957); *Problems in Addiction: Alcoholism and Narcotics* (1959); *The Clergy and the Teenager* (1961), Fordham University Press, New York, New York.

Detailed accounts of the advance preparations, the timetable, the unfolding, and the effects of summer courses organized, first of all, for the local Superiors of a teaching order of nuns (The Sisters of St. Joseph of Carondelet) and soon extended to a wider public, have been published in thirty-page brochures by Sister Annette Walters: *Report of Mental Health Training Institute* (1958) and *A Mental Health Training Institute for Administrators of Colleges, Schools, Hospitals and Charitable Institutions* (1960). National Catholic Educational Association, Sister Formation Conference, 1785 Massachusetts Avenue, N.W., Washington D.C. These booklets should be extremely useful for the organizers of similar sessions, who will also find some helpful suggestions in the *Manual of Procedures, Topics and Materials* of the "Academy of Religion and Mental Health," 1956. (16 East 34 Street, New York, New York.)

6. Two pages of instructions for composing a report on a pas-

toral interview may be found in H. Faber's *Pastoral Care and Clinical Training* (*op. cit.*, 122–123).

In our opinion, if such a report is to be of any use in discussion, it should generally be drawn up as follows:

a) A few words of introduction to explain how much was known about the counselee beforehand and to describe his general behavior at the start of the interview: demeanor, physical appearance, tone of voice, and the way in which he establishes contact.

b) Note important phases in the dialogue, respecting as far as possible the order adopted by the counselee. If possible, give the exact words used by counselor and counselee at the most crucial or critical moments in the dialogue.

c) Open or implied emotional tonalities in his attitudes toward his problems, the people in question, the counselor himself, religion, etc.

d) The counselor's final impressions and the questions he wishes to put to the group.

A different approach involves the use of the counselor's unwritten recollections of the interview. Once expressed, these memories provoke different questions from other members of the group, and the counselor then carries on the discussion with them.

7. A recorded report might also be considered, provided it was done with the consent of the counselee, who would have the opportunity of listening to the recording and erasing any sections he wished. This could then be used in a discussion concerning practical techniques. Doubtless, in a European pastoral context, the necessary conditions of assent and complete discretion for such a recording would be difficult to find.

Yet we must mention that once, thanks to the initiative of a member of one of our groups, we were able to listen to a recording made during a telephone conversation with a scrupulous counselee in which *only the counselor's words were recorded.* The result did not violate the most rigorous conditions of secrecy, and provoked a profound discussion on the deficiencies of psychological welcome and acceptance as they emerged from that conversation.

8. In an article called "L'animation pastorale et psychologique des petits groupes," in *La Nouvelle Revue Theologique* (Louvain),

January 1962, pp. 36–62, this author provides a theological and psychological description of the dynamics of these discussion and supervision groups. He also gives some practical suggestions for establishing the best possible atmosphere for ensuring that personal attitudes are brought into question. A short bibliography of articles in French, concerning the dynamics of these groups and discussion techniques, appears at the end of this author's article *Groupe sain, groupe malade*, in the *Nouvelle Revue Theologique*, June 1961, p. 616. We would also like to mention a recent work in Dutch by Mej. Dr. W. C. S. van Benthem Jutting, *Problematiek en methodiek van het groepswerk in de pastorale praktijk*, Arnhem, Van Loghum Slaterus, 1961. (Centrum voor kerkelijk-sociologisch en pastoraal-psychologisch onderzoek, Rijn en Schiekade 15, Leiden, Holland.)

APPENDIX   The Priest's Role and Parental Images

1. Father R. Hostie's excellent and precise critique in *Du mythe à la religion*, Desclée De Brouwer, 1955 (English translation, *Religion and the Psychology of Jung*, New York, Sheed & Ward, 1957), especially pages 37 to 56, should be read as an introduction to the psychological aspect of "archetypes" as primordial or archaic images, as unconscious dynamisms and as "engrams" (i.e., in their problematical relation to physiology). C. J. Jung seems to have interpreted the affective perception of the Church's role as a *maternal* archetype. Speaking about a child who had dreamed of a cathedral, which reminded him of the one at Cologne in which he once used to worship, he interpreted this majestic image as a mother-substitute: "Affectively speaking, the Church is a mother, since she acts as a spiritual substitute for the ties which once bound the child to his family." (*Ueber die Psychologie des Unbewussten*, Zurich, Rascher, 1943, 5th edition, p. 188; English translation, *Psychology of the Unconscious*, New York: Dodd, Mead, 1949.) As far as we know, Jung never considered the priest's role in this perspective.

2. Concerning the distinctive features of the paternal and maternal relationship in our West European culture (without going

into too many details), see an interesting passage in François
Duyckaerts' Introduction to his translation of Oswald Schwarz,
The Psychology of Sex, New York, Penguin, 1952; (*Psychologie
sexuelle*, Paris, Presses Universitaires de France, 1952), pp. 22–23.
Here the mother is described as the source of security, and the
father as a stimulating presence in the search for values. On the
level of his religious mediation, could the priest be considered
(analogically) as both?

3. Certain characteristics of the personal psychology of the
prophet, the priest, the intellectual (the theologian), and the
mystic are given in a descriptive rather than a scientific fashion in
Chapter XIII of W. H. Clark's textbook, *The Psychology of
Religion* (New York, Macmillan, 1958), pp. 291–306.

4. An interesting study of the magicians of primitive societies
and their relation to the superego (i.e., the elementary mechanisms
by which social pressures are inscribed in the psychic consciousness) has been made by John W. M. Whiting, "Sorcery, Sin and
the Superego: A Cross-Cultural Study of Some Mechanisms of
Social Control," in the *Nebraska Symposium on Motivation, 1959,*
(Lincoln, University of Nebraska Press, 1959), pp. 174–197, with
a discussion by Harry Levin. In France, Jacques Maitre (Director
of Research at the Centre d'Etudes Sociologiques of the C.N.R.S.)
is preparing a documentary analysis to show the psychological expectations of horoscope readers (with the claims of the writers),
and will later produce a differentiated study of certain roles expected
of priests. (To be published by Casterman in the series *Religion
et Societes.*)

5. An appropriate method (the Q-technique) for studying affinities between relations to God and paternal and maternal images is
described, together with its results, by A. Godin and M. Hallez,
"Parental Images and Divine Paternity," in *From Religious Experience to a Religious Attitude* (Brussels, Lumen Vitae Press,
1964, pp. 79–110). We found that during the early years of life
the divine image is strongly influenced by the image of the parent
of the opposite sex but that this influence declines with advancing
age and a developing spiritual life.

6. According to a preliminary investigation by Aron Wolfe Siegman, confined to seventy-nine American students (Catholics, Protestants and Jews), images strongly influenced by a parental transference tend to *diminish* with an increase in religious experience. See "La notion de Dieu et l'image du père," in *Adulte et enfant devant Dieu* (Brussels, Lumen Vitae Press, 1961, pp. 111–114).

7. Several psychologists are currently studying the genetic and phenomenological significance of the two expressions, "Our Mother the Church," and "God Our Father."

Dr. J. Lacan has the following striking observation to make concerning the oedipal phase when the small boy discovers that the object of this initial love (the mother) is subject to the law of another (the father): "He discovers the relationship between the Mother and the *Word* of the Father." Let us hope, with Dr. Serge Leclaire, in another suggestive article, that "his mother, who should be the mediatrix and the way, does not become the goal and object." ("L'obsessionnel et son desir," in *L'Evolution psychiatrique*, 1959, 3, p. 401.)

At a later age, the discovery of the relation of the Church (and perhaps of her priests) to the *word* of God might correspond to the same dialectic. This is the thesis, suggested in a highly original manner, by Dr. R. S. Lee (Pastor at Oxford): "The mother symbol which most directly interests us is the Church. . . . [Some Christians] in their conscious minds may treat the name Mother Church as a metaphor, but in their unconscious it has psychical reality, that is, the Church is their Mother. Those Christians who manifest a strong emotional anti-Papal bias, or who think of the Church of Rome as the 'scarlet woman,' betray the unconscious mother-identification by their negative reaction. They resist the idea of the Father (the Pope) having power over the Mother (the Church). Their 'Protestantism' is a reaction formation. . . . Anti-Papal convictions that are based on reasoned judgments may show even greater tenacity, but they are not accompanied by the heat of violent emotion. . . . There may be an oscillation between attraction to the Church and repulsion from it. The attraction will be to the mother, but the repulsion will be from God (the great father symbol) to whom the Church submits, or from the parson (another father substitute), who is likely to be accused of dogmatism, of authoritarianism, of smugness and other stupidities. The parson may indeed be guilty of all these, especially if he himself has a strong mother fixation, for he has gotten into the position of the father, but he may be innocent and yet accused of them." (*Freud and Christianity*, New York, Wyn, 1949, pp. 117–118.)

As can be seen in this psychological dialectic, if the role of the priest is far from clear (a paternal substitute as a representative of God *or* a maternal substitute as a member of the Church), the role of the Church-mother is definitely to lead toward God (the Father), according to St. Augustine's dictum: "Interposita matris auctoritate de patre creditur." (We believe in the father through the mediative authority of the mother: *de Utilitate Credendi*, 12, 26.) Commenting on this text, Father L. Beirnaert sees in it "man's dependence on the paternal function, although the Father can never actually appear." Together with Freud, he evokes "the victory of the spirit over the senses, which marks the passage from the matriarchate to the patriarchate: maternity is perceived through the senses, while paternity remains a conjecture in which a mystery (an absence) must be recognized at the center of reality, which reveals man to himself and to which he never stops answering." (*L'homme et son mystère*, in *Le Mystère*, Paris, Éditions Horay, 1960, p. 115).

Perhaps we could conclude by suggesting that if the Mother-image inspires man's primitive religiosity and, so to speak, his pre-history, it is the Father-image to which he is expected to relate (as an adopted son) that forms his religious, Christian history.

8. Concerning the persistence of a parental-based "superego" in the reactions of fifty Catholic girls to the image of the priest, see this author's attempt at a projective test, with its results, in "Religious Projective Pictures," in *Research in Religious Psychology*. First published in 1957 (Brussels, Lumen Vitae Press, pp. 64–78). Second edition, 1961, with a supplementary statistical analysis.

About the Author

FATHER ANDRÉ GODIN, S.J., is Professor of the Psychology of Religion and Pastoral Psychology at the International Institute of Lumen Vitae in Brussels, Belgium. A practicing psychotherapist, he was formerly Professor of Psychology at the Gregorian University in Rome, and has lectured in the United States, Canada, Mexico, and Australia.

His articles have appeared in the *Journal for the Scientific Study of Religion, Thought, Journal for Religion and Health, Religious Education,* and *Theology Digest.* He edited *Studies in Religious Psychology* and *From Religious Experience to a Religious Attitude,* and is the author of *Le dieu des parents et le dieu des enfants.*

Father Godin was born in Gembloux, Belgium, joined the Society of Jesus in 1933, and was ordained at Louvain in 1946. He studied criminal psychology under Dr. Etienne De Greeff in Brussels, and also did research in experimental psychology at Fordham University. In his concern for the development of a scientific psychology of religion, he is an advocate of more interdisciplinary research, with contributions coming both from psychoanalysis and the social sciences.